THE LETTERMAN WIT

THE LETTERMAN WIT
His Life and Humor

Bill Adler

Carroll & Graf Publishers, Inc.
New York

Copyright © 1994 by Bill Adler

First Carroll & Graf edition 1994
First trade paperback edition 1995

Carroll & Graf Publishers, Inc.
260 Fifth Avenue
New York, NY 10001

Library of Congress Cataloging-in-Publication Data

Adler, Bill.
    The Letterman wit : his life and humor / Bill Adler.—1st ed.
Carroll & Graf ed.
        p.   cm.
    ISBN 0-7867-0210-9
    1. Letterman, David.   2. Television personalities—United States—
Biography.   3. Comedians—United States—Biography.   I. Title.
PN1992.4.L39A34   1995
791.45'028'092—dc20
    [B]   94-7140
                                                                        CIP

Manufactured in the United States of America

10   9   8   7   6   5   4   3   2   1

Table of Contents

THE LETTERMAN WIT

CHAPTER ONE
Broad Ripple Days

When David Letterman was about eight years old he was just beginning to set himself apart from his peer group of eight-year-olds. He looked no different from any of the other kids in the Broad Ripple section of Indianapolis, Indiana, but in his psyche he was developing into what would become a jokester and buffoon in his college years and a world-famous talk-show host in his maturity.

"A bunch of us were playing on a backyard swing set," a neighbor of David's, Pam Frost, recalled. She remembered that even then, back in the 1950's, Dave was a great kidder. But this episode in the swing went *beyond* simple kidding.

He pumped himself up higher and higher in the swing, until he was going as fast as he could. Then, at the peak of the swing out front, he simply slid off it and fell to the ground.

"When he landed," Frost said, "he broke his arm." She thought it might have been the first of what David Letterman might later call a "stupid human trick"—a corollary of his "stupid pet tricks" that became a key element of his success in the late-night talk-show business.

For the record, David Michael Letterman was born on April 12, 1947, in Indianapolis, Indiana. His parents were Joseph and Dorothy Letterman, who owned a house in a section of the city called Broad Ripple. It was a typically post-World War II house on a small lot in the midst of hundreds of other houses on small lots.

Joseph Letterman was the son of a former coal miner who had escaped the mines in the East and had come west to become a farmer in the countryside of Indiana. Joseph did not become a farmer, however; instead, he opened up a flower shop in Broad Ripple. It would later become the first FTD in the Indianapolis area.

But he had decided to become a quasi-farmer through an interest in growing things. What he liked to plant and grow were trees. He planted dogwoods all around the area in Broad Ripple—in people's yards, in parks, and in vacant lots.

There were three children—two girls and one boy. David was the middle sibling, bracketed in between two girls, Gretchen and Janice. The sisters did well in school, especially Gretchen; David did not perform academically as well as they did. But it was obvious that he was intelligent.

The children attended Public School 55, which was well within walking distance. There David made friends with several of the boys, but did not become any kind of playground leader or classroom star. If anything, he was the exact opposite of a star.

As he progressed through childhood, he became something of a joker, as illustrated in the swing episode. More than that, he soon evinced a humorous approach to life. For that he had his grandfather on his mother's side to thank.

"My mother's father was a very funny man—a real smart-ass, but irresistible," he said. The old man had an attitude about him that was comic in the extreme. When David was a small boy, his grandfather took him out hunting watermelons. Watermelons, the old man said, were very tricky. They knew you were coming. It was tough to stalk them and find them where you could pick them off the vine.

"He would have me sneak up on the watermelons, because that was the only way you could pick them. So there would be this man in his sixties and me, a little kid, tiptoeing together through the watermelon patch, and we'd finally grab one and run like hell."

The prankster in David was obviously initiated during this period of his life. It never left him entirely. Along with the prankster, the joker—the boy who slid off the swing and broke his arm—coexisted triumphantly. And so did the television viewer.

Every Sunday the Letterman family would sit down together and watch television. Sunday was the day the *Ed Sullivan Show* was on. That was the be-all and end-all of TV for the Letterman clan.

"Every Sunday night at my house we'd have dinner early, and my father would usually make soup that we wished Mom had made. You know, it was *that* kind of soup. 'Oh, thanks, Dad.' And then we finished dinner and watched the *Ed Sullivan Show*. Whether we wanted to or not. Whether we enjoyed it or not. That was my first lesson in show business. I don't think anybody in the house particularly *enjoyed* it. We just watched it. Maybe that's the purpose of television. You just turn it on and watch it whether you want to or not."

It was more fun to play with the other kids, anyway. TV was an indoor sport, and David was an outdoor boy at that time. With a neighbor, David decided to build themselves a wood-and-tar tree house made out of cardboard and tarpaper at the back end of the neighbor's property.

The neighbors were solicitous. Tree houses were a universally accepted form of youthful craftsmanship. No one seemed concerned when the boys would climb up into the cardboard box and settle down for the late afternoon.

At about the same time, a number of automobiles became engaged in near collisions in the area of the tree house. A neighbor became suspicious and began to investigate. And it was a good thing he did so. What he uncovered was the beginning of a somewhat dangerous recreation.

The mother of one of David's buddies explained later: "The boys were using their high position in the tree to shine the sun off a mirror and into the eyes of approaching motorists!"

Nothing like seasoning their recreation with a bit of danger!

The upshot of the episode was that the boys were banned from using the tree house, except on overcast and rainy days.

By the end of his grade-school career David had become more of an activist than he ever was before. He put people down at the drop of a hat. He was a whiz at repartee, never at a loss for the perfect squelch.

It did not improve his classroom demeanor any when he began to spice up his themes, either. For one paper he was assigned to do, about an important event in an individual's life, he wrote an ode to a man who had killed himself by swallowing an enormous quantity of paper towels.

The teacher was not amused.

Even in grade school, David was never above ribbing any of the Establishment institutions around him, even such a sacred rite as a graduation dance held for the eighth graders when they "graduated" from grammar school. To startle everyone and point out that David Letterman did not always abide by popular and acceptable mores, he appeared dressed up in a madras sport coat, Bermuda shorts, and ridiculous knee socks.

Bill Sellery, a friend at Public School 55, recalled: "The adults were horrified. But David didn't care what anyone else thought. He did what he felt like doing."

In 1961, David entered Broad Ripple High School along with several hundred other freshmen. For the next four years David struggled as best he could through his high school years. They were not particularly happy ones. He was himself, and he made no attempt to reinitiate himself as someone else just to be popular.

The kids at Broad Ripple High used to think they were really raising hell when they piled into a car with a six-pack of beer, and cruised through the 'hoods in the late night hours.

"In high school, I was never with smart kids. I was never with great athletes. There was a small pocket of people I hung out with, and all we did was make fun of good-looking people, smart kids, and great athletes."

David's father suffered financial reverses in the 1950's. "There was a lot of financial tension around the house," David recalled.

David Letterman reacted in a typically Midwestern way: he got a job in the afternoons. And so for his four years at Broad Ripple High, David did not participate in many extracurricular activities at school. Instead, he worked all four years at the Atlas Super Market in Broad Ripple. This was an independent market run by a man named Sidney Maurer. Maurer made it a policy to hire local kids to do the scut work at the store, always having from six to eight of them around in the afternoons.

In a way, it was the customers at Atlas who were the brunt of David's pranks rather than the high school students who were his peers.

After David had mastered the art of sacking groceries—that included putting them in the paper sacks and then in taking the sacks out to the car for the shoppers—he was promoted to stocking the shelves. Finally, he began cleaning up the store. In the end, he acted as a kind of standby always ready to fill in during an emergency.

Beyond that, he was made checker at the cash register.

But those details were irrelevant. What he *really* did was act like David Letterman was supposed to act. Doug Templeton, a coworker who went to school with him, recalled one trick that David pulled.

"He told all the shoppers to write their names on their receipts and stuff them into a box. There would be a raffle on Saturday and the winner would get a 1962 Super Sport Automobile."

Of course there was no automobile.

"When Saturday rolled around and shoppers showed up, there wasn't any raffle or prize. Some [people] were pretty angry." To put it mildly.

Another prank at the store had the name David Letterman stamped all over it. One Friday he announced that there would be a mah-jongg tournament to be held at one o'clock in the afternoon on Sunday. "You won't want to miss it!"

He was right. Many of the people who came to the store did not want to miss anything, even a mah-jongg tournament.

"But a handful [of the less wary] showed up on Sunday . . . to find the store closed."

Not all his pranks were confined to the supermarket. In spite of his afternoon job, David did get on the basketball team. Eric Sander, a classmate, recalled that the coach was a rather typical high school coach—a muscle-bound jock who spoke in a "dese" and "dose" jargon to give himself a tough-guy (and false) image.

David used to revel in his ability to mock the coach by imitating his exaggerated and ridiculous stance. He would make a face, twisting his mouth and chin out of line and saying deep down in his throat, "All right, youse guys, dese guys we're playin' next is gonna be tough ghees to beat, ya know?"

Even at that age David had an attitude that pierced the phony facades people put up to hide themselves behind.

Although he was a humorist who could make his close friends laugh, he made no attempt in those days to widen his area of friends. He rarely performed in school plays or on the stage: only in one musical.

"That would have been too nerve-wracking. And I felt I looked so awful. I was much too shy to perform. I was looking through my high school yearbook recently. We all looked like guys who'd be hanging around with John Hinckley. I mean, basically, everybody in high school looks like a duck."

When things got dull at the supermarket, David would get on the store intercom and announce that there was a fire drill in order to prepare customers for the real thing. He would use a serious, official voice, warning people: "Proceed in an orderly fashion to the parking lot. No rushing, please."

Everyone would follow his instructions to a T. And, of course, they were pretty angry when they found out it was all a joke. But no one ever did anything to David.

Templeton recalled a time when David Letterman found a partially open box of corn flakes in the pile he was stacking on the shelves. After he had finished, he took the box back to the produce section where some of the workers were shucking corn for the vegetable stands. Out of sight, he emptied the box and stuffed it full of corn husks and tassels. Then he put the box back on the shelf.

"A week later, an irate customer came in demanding to see the store owner. The guy said, 'What the heck is this, Sid—look in this cereal box!' "

A moment later, the intercom boomed out: "David Letterman, come to my office. Right now!"

But David did not lose his job. He was not even threatened. Sidney Maurer was an easygoing person who actually got a kind of kick out of his gags.

"David certainly had a wacky sense of humor," Maurer said recently.

Maurer recalled another gag in which David figured. He was instructed by a straight-arrow assistant manager to stack some cans up for a display. When the somewhat unimaginative assistant returned to see if the work was done, he found that it certainly *was* done—done to a crisp. David had stacked the cans all the way to the ceiling in a wall of merchandise so that no one could remove one can without forcing the whole display to tumble down.

"The assistant manager didn't think it was funny," Maurer said. "But I did. I ran a laid-back store, and it was just harmless fun."

High school days were not days of romance for David Letterman. He was not a popular item with the girls in class. Because he was not in the general swim, he was forced to hang around with other teenagers who were not popular with them, either. Instead of trying to get dates with any of the better-looking girls, David and his gang would slip out into the streets and throw eggs at the girls' houses.

But David never considered himself a "class clown," as many incipient comics have been. When asked whether or not he was a class clown, David repied: "No. Most of the class clowns in my high school are doing time now."

Tom Ley, a high school classmate, remembered one specific comic trick that Letterman was already beginning to perfect even in those early years. He would always pay a great deal of attention to details, especially when it came to teasing his friends. If, for example, someone had gotten a too-ambitious haircut that made his ears stand out, David would bring up the fact and comment on it in a humorous and kidding way.

"Had your ears lowered, Tom?"

But that was not the essence of the jest. He would later *return* to the detail time and time again. His insistence on going back to the original jibe about the haircut and the ears seemed to make the haircut funnier and funnier.

The cream of the jest, however, was the fact that each time David *mentioned* the haircut, he would come at it in a new and novel way.

"I guess you walk *sideways* in a strong wind, is that it, Tom?"

"First of the tall ships in today's parade, Tom?"

"How are the satellite dishes working for long-distance reception, Tom?"

It was not only the repetition of the jest but the wide-ranging originality of the ensuing comments that in the end made the haircut a risible subject—and not merely the simple idea of the gibe.

Many years later, in 1984, when David Letterman had his own *Late Night* show on NBC, he was invited on the Phil Donahue show. There Donahue rigged up a *This Is Your Life* segment that included a man named Gene Poston, who had been Letterman's drama coach at Broad Ripple High School. But it was not David's drama that fascinated, but the fact that Poston mentioned to Donahue that David had been a "hall monitor" in high school.

Donahue was astounded. Hall monitor! "Do you know what we used to call those people?" he asked his audience.

Someone shouted, "Yes."

"What?" Donahue asked.

"Finks," shouted a woman in the audience.

David Letterman immediately responded. "I take exception with this woman claiming I was a fink. The hall monitor, at least at Broad Ripple—perhaps Gene here can back me up on this—we took these positions just to get out of any organized classroom activity. We could go sit in a darkened hallway and doze or do whatever. We didn't fink, ma'am, no. It was just a short vacation."

Later on, as Poston continued to chat about Broad Ripple High School, David Letterman broke in with a wide smile: "Any talk of naming a wing after me, Gene?"

"Not yet, Dave," Poston answered. "Hold on."

David's father had a heart attack while David was still in high school. He died a few years later. It was a sad blow to him, although he joked about it sometime later.

"My mother's still working," he told a job interviewer in that pseudoserious style of his, "but my dad is dead, so he does precious little anymore."

He was able to retain that spark of youthful prankishness when he began to render his jokes in words rather than in actions.

CHAPTER TWO
At Ball State

As David Letterman learned to verbalize his antics and make his joshing somewhat more subtle—but still as pointed as before—he realized that he had uncovered a potential in himself that he had never before recognized.

The fact was, as everyone else knew already, he was a born talker, a conversationalist, a man of words. As he looked back on his many straight-faced lies—his announcements of fire drills, his phony mah-jongg tournaments, his fake raffles—he knew that he had become a persuasive and convincing speaker.

If he could accomplish so much by deliberately lying to someone, why should he worry about his future? If he had a gift of gab, as his Indiana contemporaries might put it, why hide it under a bushel?—to mix a metaphor or two.

"There was a period in high school, and maybe that's when it comes for everybody, when you sort of had to figure out who you were," he recalled later. "You think, 'Well, I'm not fitting in with the group, the really desirable blue-chip group, and I'm not fitting into that group.' And then you start to examine your own inventory and think, 'Is there anything I can do that is going to make me desirable or make me different?' "

That question was answered in his mind when he remembered something that had always interested him. "When I was a kid," he said later, "I was aware of Arthur Godfrey's daytime show, and Garry Moore, and I found it fascinating to see these people sit at little desks and have these microphones in front of them and talk, and I thought, 'This is amazing,' and I sort of would pretend to be on TV or radio and thought, 'This would be great,' and then I forgot all about it until I got into high school and took a speech class, the first class I didn't have to work too hard to get good grades in."

And that was when lightning struck.

"For the first time in my formal academic experience there was a subject that seemed to come easily to me, more easily than algebra or geometry or shop. I was not very bright, and may not be very bright in the rest of my life, but at that time it was clear to me that this was something to remember. That this was a valuable lesson."

And so David Letterman thought, "Now the trick is, how do I find out how to get paid to do this?" But then he remembered that he possessed one other talent he could put to use. "I realized I had one little tool: I could make people laugh. The problem was, where? How? What am I going to do? Join the circus? In the meantime, my family was convinced I was going to go through life being a wise-ass. I wasn't in the smart classes in high school. I couldn't do math, I couldn't learn German. So instead of college courses, I was getting put into things like General Merchandising.

"Then one day I realized I was as smart as my friends." After all, he was in a speech class. He thought, "Wait a minute! I can actually get a grade here, just standing up and telling stories!" That was a real insight to him. "How do you apply this?" he wondered.

"And then I found out you could study broadcasting in college, and I thought, 'Holy cow! There you go! It's a miracle. What's next?' And what was next was figuring out how to get on the radio."

But first, of course, he had to leap that giant hurdle—how to get into college with his somewhat anemic grade average.

In effect, he had everything figured out about his future except how to get there.

His first choice was Indiana University at Bloomington. That was the best state school and a good college where he could get the required university education to go on into the communications business. Even if he was able to con his way into the university, he would have to maintain a C average during his freshman year. Knowing his shortcomings, Letterman decided he could not risk that.

And so he lowered his sights just a bit and applied to Ball State University, which was a part of the Indiana state system. The college was located in Muncie, which was not far away—no more than an hour's drive—and he was accepted. He started college in September 1965.

There was no "Ball State," of course. "Ball" referred to the family that had manufactured Ball canning jars nearby for many years. And "State" meant that the college was part of the state system.

Muncie was not much different from Indianapolis, except that there were a lot more farms and the area was principally agricultural rather than manufacturing or industrial.

It was hardly a college town, even though Ball State University was located there. The campus was strung out along a couple of blocks on Muncie's two main drags. The architecture was Midwestern utilitarian, built in the 1940's, 1950's, and 1960's.

From the beginning, David Letterman thrived on the collegiate atmosphere of small-town Muncie. While he never flourished on the atmosphere at Broad Ripple High School, he did find a home for himself at Ball State. In fact, one of the school's unwritten mottos was once enunciated by a member of the faculty in these words:

"We do our best job here when we don't destroy what [the students] have coming in before we let them out."

And at Ball State, the young David Letterman did find himself.

At the same time, he managed to exult in the typical things that college students the world over exult in.

"One of the remarkable things about being nineteen is that you can break open a case of warm beer at midnight and still be wide-eyed and alert for your eight A.M. class. And that gave me the false impression that my life would always be like that."

Having already decided what he would do, he selected a major in radio and television. And from the beginning he found that he was a somewhat better student than he had been led to believe he was in Broad Ripple. He did not have any trouble in his grades, getting a B average during his freshman and sophomore years. In his junior and senior years his grade average declined—because of the extracurricular work he was involved in—to about a C average.

His extracurricular activities were focused on the reason he had come to college in the beginning. His first job was in 1967, at the student radio station, WBST. It was obvious from his diction and the way he spoke that he was a natural for radio. He was one of the first selected from the year's list of undergraduates under consideration.

At the time, a new manager had been hired to run the station. The university felt that the operation had been slipshod and ramshackle during its earlier years. The idea was to slick it up and make it more "professional."

That was not an easy job. The station broadcast on ten watts, with a strange lineup of programs that concentrated mostly on classical music. The pay for student disc jockeys was $1.25 an hour. For that $1.25 they were required always to announce the name of the piece and the composer correctly.

Selected as student manager by the Ball State University faculty was an upwardly mobile go-getter who was determined to put an end to the sophomoric posturing and clowning that went on in the studio and seeped out onto the air.

David Letterman's gig stretched from noon to three in the afternoon, and in that three-hour window, classical music predominated. He knew little about that type of music, and cared even less about learning what it was all about.

As a result, sometimes his announcements left a bit to be

desired—if you considered his pronouncements from the standpoint of a professor of musicology. What he *liked* about the job was that he was talking, and earning money doing it.

"I used to have a radio program on WBST and that was just the best. That was my first outlet, my first place to just go and talk, and I loved it." Even then, David had picked up the habit of punning ("best" to echo "WBST"). And his humor was always there, waiting to surface at any moment.

One afternoon it did surface—and surface dramatically. And the student manager was there to hear it. The selection itself was an easy one—Claude Debussy's *Clair de Lune.* He even gave the composer's last name the perfect French twist: the long "oo" with the lips puckered up prissily.

Having done that, he simply could not resist adding in the low-voiced confidential manner of Milton Cross describing the action at the Metropolitan Opera on radio:

"You know the de Lune sisters. There was Clair, there was Mabel. . . ."

And then the instrumental.

It was the end of the job at WBST.

But radio was alive and well in other parts of the campus. In a broom closet of the men's dorm, a group of students ran a pirate radio station, WAGO. This five-watt station competed for listeners using pop music and a format that dealt frequently in blue humor.

David was not comfortable with jokes of that nature. When he went on the air he generally steered clear of all such material. What he did was usually joke about the town of Muncie, in which the college was located. It was a classic archetype of a small town.

His own private life consisted mostly of cracking the books just enough to get by, and hanging around with the rest of the students. What he loved to do was to sit with friends drinking beer out of the bottle and kidding each other.

The kidding was not mild. It was virulent stuff sometimes. But David was honing his own sense of humor and exploring new ways to bedevil his peers.

And at bedevilment, David Letterman was without equal.

He had pledged Sigma Chi Fraternity, and his Sigma Chi brothers were the obvious targets of his pestiferousness. They were close by, and they were vulnerable.

Doug Deputy, a fraternity brother, remembered one incident that had the signature of David Letterman written all over it.

"There was a guy in the house who was a football player. Dave somehow talked him into shaving his head. Then he wanted him to paint his head blue so David could point him out as the world's largest ballpoint pen. Or something like that."

"The big thing," David remembered, "was to get as drunk as possible as early in the day as possible so you would be conscious for the least amount of time. College enables young people to be stupider longer with minimal jeopardy. In fact, that was on the shield of my fraternity in Latin: 'Stupider Longer.' "

David was becoming a professional talker by now. It was never a surprise to see a group of students gathered around him in the halls or on the campus. Students, one professor noted, would always be laughing and waiting expectantly to hear what he had to say.

And if there was any kind of misadventure, he was usually at the center of it. One of the department heads at Ball State took a group of his students on a field trip to New York to visit CBS. "On the train trip back to Indiana, Dave and some other guys got off somewhere in darkest Ohio, got snockered and almost missed the train," one of the group said. "[The department head] was not too pleased."

This was the activist 1960's, but the urgency of activism was not all that apparent at Ball State—at least to David Letterman.

"All over the United States, protest," David recalled. "Kent State was not that far away, and even Bloomington, the campus down there, was a hotbed of protest. But not Ball State. We were pretty well protected. Quite honestly, the only protest that I ever was involved in was, we thought we maybe could get the cafeteria cooks to wear hairnets."

But things were not always so isolated. "I was hardly aware of the Vietnam War until a friend of mine flunked out and was drafted and was dead like *that*. One day, here's a guy setting fire to the housemother's panty hose, and the next day, he's *gone*. That got my attention."

Jeff Lewis, one of Dave Letterman's fraternity brothers at Sigma Chi, was invited to the 1984 Phil Donahue talk show mentioned earlier to be part of Letterman's past.

"Jeff," Donahue asked Lewis, "was David Letterman popular with girls? Was it one steady girl? Did he have a lot of girlfriends? Did he get home on time at night? Give us the whole picture."

Lewis blinked. "Gee. That's a lot." He thought a moment, looking at Letterman, who was giving him a steely-eyed glance. "No. He was not popular with the girls. He had one steady girlfriend and he wasn't popular with her."

The audience laughed. Donahue turned to Letterman. "Jeff hasn't changed, has he?" Letterman started to speak, but then demurred.

Lewis said, "I helped him get home late past the hours many times. So he didn't get home on time."

Realizing he had held his silence long enough, the subject of the comic bombardment asked Donahue in a slightly plaintive way: "Is this one of those special ninety-minute shows, Phil?"

Donahue asked Lewis, "Did you think this chap was going to hit it like this?"

"No doubt about it," Lewis said simply.

"You *really* did think so?"

"Without question."

"You're the kind of buddy to have."

Letterman agreed. "He was the kind of buddy to have in college. This man was *the* Mr. Campus. This man was president of—anything we had he was president of. He was a very astute politician and pursued a career in politics. This was your Blue Chip Mr. Big Man on Campus. So this was a great friend to have."

Lewis reached into his pocket, deadpan. "Here's your money, Dave."

"You pretty much ran things in Muncie," Letterman reminded him.

"It was a short career."

Donahue asked, "Was it an *Animal House* thing or—?"

Lewis nodded. "At times it was even funnier."

The "one steady girlfriend" Letterman had, mentioned by Jeff Lewis, was named Michelle Cook. She, too, was a student at Ball State, majoring in music. She was somewhat quiet—quite a contrast to David—and she was serious—again, a contrast to David. But like David she was tall—about six feet—and quite attractive.

As was his wont, David teased her unmercifully about her height. He compared her to a tree in the arboretum, even accused her of being in charge of changing light bulbs in the men's gym. In spite of this somewhat tasteless jibing, she liked him. Even fell in love with him.

They decided to marry while they were still in college. That meant that David Letterman had to live by a whole new set of rules. He had to support himself and his wife. But she, too, pitched in.

Michelle became a waitress in a Muncie restaurant. David got a job at a local radio station. They were out in the real world, with real-world problems. At WERK, David began as a substitute for Tom Cochrun, a regular announcer who had also gone to Ball State. Cochrun was in Europe at the time.

David got the job and played records and read the news. In this job, since a lot depended on it—money and a wife and square meals—he did not humor himself on the job at the expense of his employment there.

When Cochrun came back, Dave was out of work again. However, he had made a good impression at WERK and got a job at WLWI-TV (Channel 13) in Indianapolis on the strength of it.

"Every half hour, I'd give the station's call sign and also announce every public service message." David thought he was doing a terrific job there. "Here I was at nineteen, talking to central Indiana. Of course, central Indiana wasn't listening."

He graduated from Ball State in 1970. Later, quite candidly, he said that Ball State had helped him recognize the fact that he could, indeed, make a living in broadcasting.

As the host of the *Late Night Show* in 1985, David Letterman showed his appreciation to Ball State University by establishing a funded scholarship for a telecommunications major. He also gave $24,285 to the radio and television department to purchase audio and video equipment.

What made the scholarship just a little *different*—and even got it mentioned in a news story in 1990 about unusual scholarships—was the fact that the only students who were eligible for the scholarship were students in telecommunications with a C average.

"Letterman considered himself a C student," a spokesperson told the press. "He doesn't want A students."

In fact, outside the studio that was refurbished by Letterman's grant there is a bronze plaque that, to this day, reads:

"Dedicated to all the C students before and after me." Signed: "David M. Letterman."

CHAPTER THREE
Start-Up

"I remember being surprised when I got out of college that the real world was unlike the fraternity house in one very important way," David Letterman told *Playboy* magazine. "The people I was working with weren't drinking as much beer as I was. So I'd find the two or three guys who still were and they would be my friends. And we had plenty of fun being young adults loose on the town. We'd just go out every night after work and drink."

Of course drinking beer with his friends was in no way the most important feature of his social life. As a newlywed husband, he was spending most of his quality time getting acquainted with Michelle and trying to cope with married life and its many diverse and complex problems.

After graduating from Ball State University, David and Michelle were faced with a number of important decisions. The most important, of course, was getting work to keep themselves afloat. And the next most important was finding a decent place to live.

As for employment, David did luck out on that. He had worked for Channel 13 during the summer, and when he went to management and requested a job interview, they immediately obliged him. Because of his previous work he felt that he would be immediately hired as a permanent announcer.

Nothing could have been further from the truth. He was hired, all right—but as a *temporary.*

"It was interesting. I got that job [originally] as a summer vacation relief announcer and every year they would have auditions to replace me. I went through five years of two or three times a week watching them audition my replacement. And—believe it or not—they never found anybody who was even that good!"

At least the problem of *employment* was solved. Since his job was in Indianapolis, he decided to move back to his hometown with Michelle and find a place to live. They rented an apartment very close to the Broad Ripple neighborhood. There was one drawback. This new neighborhood was devoted almost exclusively to seniors who were on their last legs or in their wheelchairs.

David had never settled for the conventional, and he did not do so even during his early years of marriage. The house and the car syndrome for newlyweds was out. Instead of a house, they rented an apartment; instead of a car, they both bought bicycles.

It was the early seventies then, and David was still wearing a beard—a beard he had adopted as a somewhat outward manifestation of the hippie culture that he had almost totally eschewed or ignored. The beard he sported was not actually a very kempt one; it was a mess, actually—untrimmed, bushy, and explosive.

Nor was his hair much better. When he tried to slick it down, it always got out of control and stood up on its cowlick own. When he was not at work, he liked to roust about in ragged jeans, sweatshirts with the sleeves cut off, and a seriously ancient racing cap.

As for the social life of the Lettermans, he and Michelle did not entertain much, but when they did, they never bothered to make a big thing out of it. Yet when they gave a party, the people who attended remembered them as gracious hosts. Actually, David was a much more gracious host than gracious guest.

A story about him as guest circulated for some time during the early 1970's. He and Michelle were invited to the house of Tom Cochrun, the radio announcer he had been hired to replace during the summer months at WERK. Cochrun had attended Ball State University, too. Also invited to the Cochrun place were a number of young people from Indianapolis, most of them intelligent, upwardly mobile, educated, and eager.

However bright they were, to David's eyes they were astonishingly similar in attire and appearance. Shortly after taking a long and assessing look at them, he vanished into the Cochrun bathroom.

There he moistened his hair, and with a comb slicked it down as close to his skull as he could. Then he stripped to his T-shirt, rolled a pack of cigarettes in the sleeve in imitation of servicemen visiting the hellholes of the world, and strolled out into the living room again.

He played the assumed role for the rest of the evening. And, the story went, he fooled a number of people who did not know him in his ordinary guise.

David was maturing in his role of satirist. The T-shirt role was, in retrospect, a Lettermanesque performance—a slight cock of the snook at the upwardly mobile and impressionable junior executives of Indianapolis. And, in addition, it was an obvious statement of derision made by a much less obvious satirist.

By donning the familiar costume of someone from another group or society—a roustabout serviceman—Letterman was pointing up the absurdity of the costume the go-getters in the junior executive corps assumed. He was making a statement, perhaps, about "the enormity of their conformity," as W. S. Gilbert (of the firm of Gilbert and Sullivan) might put it in one of his famous rhymes.

David's outdoor recreation at the time was mostly concerned with action on the local baseball diamond, where he always supported the local teams.

Eventually, he and Michelle got tired of the small apartment they lived in and moved to a bigger place. They were really only trading an old geriatricsville for a newer geriatricsville somewhat removed from the old one. The Lettermans still used their bicycles to get to and from the center of the city.

But David Letterman's quirky psyche was always at work underneath whatever exterior he used to hide it. He soon became restless with the bicycles and purchased a canoe. The city of Indianapolis is split in the middle by a canal that begins at the end of the White River at a dam and wanders through the city, ending in the heart of the downtown area.

After a while, rowing the canoe palled on him and he bought himself a red pickup truck. And in that he wound up his commuting days at Channel 13. He considered those days in Indianapolis as quite conventional in nature, although he himself was as unconventional as ever.

On a professional level, he felt that his work on television was not too confining at all.

"It was great, the best experience anybody could have," he said. "It was like graduate school—maybe better." What he meant but did not say aloud was that the job allowed him to hone his own sense of humor and gave him a great deal of on-air experience while he became more at ease and adept at appearing in front of the television camera.

At WLWI, Channel 13, he was assigned to three specific chores always given beginners at the station. He was the host of the late-night movie; he interviewed 4-H kids on a Saturday afternoon show; and he was substitute weatherman on the weekend news programs.

What he did with these three spots told a lot about what David Letterman might be going to do in the future on television.

First of all he made up a name for the late-night movie. He called the show *Freeze-Dried Movies*. The picture would start at 2 A.M. and go on until it ended. Letterman had no idea that he would someday be starting his own show on national television at 12:30 A.M. in a slot comparable to that of his crazy *Freeze-Dried Movies.*

Because of the time slot in the wee small hours of morning, he knew he could do just about anything he wanted to in introducing the movies or in ignoring them completely. And, since there were no rigid rules to adhere to in that remote area of TV, he began involving other members of the station in whatever antics he could dream up.

In one instance, he started a local telethon to get money to help out an ancient fighter who was long in the tooth and far over the hill. A visitor to the show one night was dressed in such an outlandish suit that Letterman insisted on putting him on the show so the viewers could take a look at him. On the show's second week, Letterman celebrated the "tenth anniversary of *Freeze-Dried Movies.*"

As for his interviews with the kids in the 4-H club on Saturdays, most of his hosting involved exchanges with the children. Although he still loved to tease his peers, he did not particularly like to tease children. There seemed to him to be little to tease them about, since they were at best unsophisticated and unaware of their own youthful indiscretions. Besides, he did not really want to hurt their feelings—and so he more or less pulled in his horns and went easy on them.

He called the 4-H show *Clover Power.*

But his favorite time slot was his weekend stint as weatherman for the Indianapolis metropolitan area. Actually, it was his most prestigious role. More people listened to the news than any of the shows he put on. Besides, Indianians are always interested in the weather. (The crops, of course.)

It was here in his on-air incarnation that he was able to Lettermanize what he was doing to the nth degree. His theory was that the weather could only be announced, with all the highs and lows mentioned and the temperatures stated, "so many times before you go insane." In his own case, he said, it took about two weeks before insanity arrived and claimed him.

A tape of one of his early broadcasts showed him struggling with the material. His odd sense of humor made what he was saying immensely funny to him, although not to everyone else.

"Nothing is going to happen to us as far as weather is concerned," he said. "It's going to be just like it was yesterday, and just like it is today, and it's going to be like that tomorrow and again on Tuesday, because nothing's going on."

It was like that day after day. Eventually, he admitted, "I started clowning."

That meant drawing funny objects on the maps. He invented mind-boggling disasters in far-off places. He came up with names of cities that did not exist.

"I made up my own measurements for hail, and said that hailstones the size of canned hams were falling," he told *People* magazine.

On one memorable occasion, he announced that a tropical storm had just been upgraded by the National Weather Service to hurricane status. He then paused and offered heartfelt congratulations to the storm on having its career advanced on national television.

The weather map one night unintentionally left off the state of Georgia. Letterman winged it with that one. He informed his audience in his off-beat way that the U.S. government had traded that state for the country of Iran, and all its citizens. He informed his viewers that soon that country and all its people would be placed where Georgia had been.

Later on there was another Weather Service error. "Take a look at the cloud cover photograph of the United States made earlier today," he enjoined his viewers. "I think you'll see that once again we have fallen to the prey of political dirty dealings. And right now you can see what I'm talking about. The higher-ups have removed the border between Indiana and Ohio, making it one giant state. Personally, I'm against it."

So was everyone else in Indiana.

About the little stars that the weather map showed to indicate snowflakes, he suggested that people at home might like to cut that portion out of their picture and use it to make doilies.

Temperature readings lent themselves often to Lettermanesque jokes:

"Muncie, 42. Anderson, 44." Letterman: "A close game, that one."

Nevertheless, he was feeling the pressure of imminent disaster. He knew that Indianians did not take their weather facts lightly. "People got disgusted and complained. I was asked to tone it down a bit."

He did. But not much.

Anyone studying him could see that his "clowning," as he called it, was more than simple clowning in its accepted sense. In inventing weird disasters and making up places that did not exist he was indulging himself in another facet of his complicated humor. It was "nonsense"—nothing more and nothing less. And the nonsense that David found most compatible with his sense of humor was fragile, soap-bubble thin, and as evanescent as butterfly wings. It was strongly reminiscent of the nonsense verse of that great nineteenth-century British humorist and illustrator, Edward Lear.

Even so, Dave was getting just a bit bored with his job on television. He could go on forever, of course—but for what purpose? Was the weather on weekends, stupid movies in the wee small hours, and adolescents with green thumbs enough for him?

"I could have become one of any number of guys who have stayed on in any market of the country," he said, using the term "market" for the area in which Channel 13 was viewed. "There are guys who have been on twenty-five years."

He did not like the picture he was seeing in his mind of his declining years. He decided that he did not intend to stay working forever in Indianapolis. But how could he get a job somewhere else?

He began to produce his own promotion tapes and sent them out with, at first, great enthusiasm. This waned after a couple of years that proved totally unproductive.

He nosed around in the industry. The obvious way to succeed was to go up and up in television. He had already made a breakthrough from radio to television. He ought to continue to the stratosphere in television.

But there was always a kind of perversity in David Letterman. The truth of the matter was that he was getting minimum exposure on TV, with the weekend weather the only thing that let him be seen by more than a handful of insomniacs. On radio, the sky was the limit. Everybody had a radio. And radio waves traveled farther than TV signals, expanding the size of an audience.

For Letterman, there was a tremendous advantage to radio. Nobody was watching you while you performed. David Letterman was still haunted by a shyness that he could not control—perhaps never would be able to control.

He auditioned. In 1974, WNTS, a radio station in Indianapolis, hired him to try out as a talk-show host. The station was trying to corner the market by hiring a number of beginners to train in the arcane arts of interviewing over the air.

Letterman was assigned to an afternoon show, one of the prime-time slots, where he played host to a call-in show. From the beginning, Letterman realized that he had allowed himself to be led up the primrose path of false hopes.

"You have to have somebody who is fairly knowledgeable, fairly glib, possessing a natural interest in a number of topics," Letterman said. He was the wrong choice in radio. He felt he was miscast. He hated the job. "I don't care about politics; I don't care about the world economy; I don't care about Martians cleaning our teeth."

What he wanted to do at the end of the day was go home and drink beer. And so he began doing what he had always done. He started to announce fictional sporting events. One of the sports he invented, according to *Rolling Stone,* had a ball that was supposedly eight feet in diameter. The object was to get the immense ball out of the stadium and into the opposing team's bus. He would spend minutes on the air expounding on the details of the nonexistent actions of the nonexistent players in this nonexistent nonsense game.

He was tired of not getting anywhere at WNTS. He finally decided to take a flier and go out to Los Angeles. That was where the action was. Michelle was enthusiastic about the proposed move.

"She started running around and packing the dishes and telling me this time we were really going to do it," Letterman remembered. "She was very supportive." He paused. "I knew I was going to fail."

CHAPTER FOUR
The Flop-Sweats

Many times in the following months David Letterman thought about what he had said to himself back in Indianapolis before leaving for the West Coast: "I knew I was going to fail."

The way things turned out, he might have put a curse upon himself by thinking those thoughts, for the move to Los Angeles was an unmitigated and absolute disaster. Of course, the way was scattered with a break or two—in the professional sense—but in general the world of David Letterman seemed to be imploding upon itself.

The disaster did not occur overnight. It was slow in building; but it was incxorable. The Lettermans arrived in Los Angeles in 1975. It was a this-and-that game for months. But in 1977, the full import of David's fate was becoming obvious.

On a personal level, the marriage that had begun so brightly in Muncie on the college campus was in big trouble. It was suffering from terminal ennui. For a long time things kept going from bad to worse, but by 1977 it was all over. Everything that had been good between David and Michelle fell apart.

To be honest about it, David did get gigs here and there—nothing big, a kernel of corn here, a kernel there. He worked at night as well as in the daytime. He was on show-biz time (twenty-four hours a day) and Michelle was on business time (nine-to-five).

She had secured a position as a buyer for a department store in Los Angeles. Her income was steady and substantial, enough to allow David to concentrate on the problem of getting himself going in big-time TV.

"My wife was working [during the day]. So at night she would come home and I would go out. We started not seeing each other week in and week out. . . . We just didn't know who we were."

Letterman saw another reason for the collapse of his marriage.

"Our basic problem was that we'd just gotten married too young."

There was no way out of it. The Lettermans divorced in 1977.

To David, the end of his life with Michelle was not the happy outcome of an early dream. "I was really committed, and I couldn't believe it when it came to an end."

But it did.

On a professional level, things were just a bit brighter. They were not brighter in the sense of star-bright, but they were a little more luminous at least. Early in 1977, Jack Rollins, of Rollins, Joffe, Morra & Brezner, a prestigious firm of show-biz agents, took on David Letterman as a client, and began scouting around for appearances for him.

And Dave began getting jobs, writing jokes for Bob Hope, Paul Lynde, and John Denver—among others. He appeared for a one-shot deal on television on *The Gong Show* and a program called *Rock Concert.* Then he became a regular on *The Peeping Times,* a parody of *60 Minutes.*

The week before shooting started, Letterman recalled, he got a call from a secretary at *The Peeping Times* office. "We've been trying to get hold of your agent," she told him, "but we can't reach him, so we're just going to tell you. You've got to get your teeth fixed."

Letterman was surprised, wondering what there was about his teeth that needed work. "I ran to the mirror . . . and honest to God I noticed for the first time that I have these huge spaces between my two front teeth."

He didn't want his teeth capped, and discovered that he could get what the dental profession called "inserts."

"Except that when I wore them, I couldn't speak properly. Every P just exploded into the mike."

And so he did not get his teeth fixed. The show was short-lived, anyway. The old show-biz adage—satire closes on Saturday night—proved true once again.

Having Rollins for an agent helped immeasurably. When Letterman had first hit Los Angeles, he had no contacts whatsoever. He did have an ace up his sleeve: at least, he thought so. When he was working for WNTS in Indianapolis, he had met Betty White and Allen Ludden, who occasionally visited to promote their syndicated radio show. They had invited him to look them up if he ever visited L.A.

What the two of them did for him was all they could do. They booked him as a guest on their half-hour television panel program called *What Is It?* He appeared. The audience clapped. He smiled. It was all over. Result? *Nada.*

"I originally went to Los Angeles as a writer. It's more palatable to tell your family that you're going to be a writer than it is to tell them that you're going to do stand-up comedy. They think you're looking for circus work or something like that."

When a number of other bright inspirations turned out to be duds, Letterman called upon his writing talents. The legendary Comedy Store was in its heyday. No one who was anybody in show-biz comedy had failed to make an appearance there.

Stand-up was not Letterman's first choice of work. Nor had he ever had any practice at it. Actually, there were no places in Indianapolis that dealt in that particular commodity. And so now he sat down and began writing jokes to tell at the Comedy Store.

He called his experience there "a horrible" one—"just terrible."

In his understated way he was making a point. The truth

of the matter was that he did the stand-up without injury to himself. "I wasn't a flop in that I left the stage in a conscious state," he assessed his appearance later.

But he was in no way a triumph. "I got up and said from rote the stuff I had written that day," he told *Newsweek* magazine. "To dead silence."

That was not quite true. Letterman was putting himself down as he generally did. Another up-and-coming comedian, Jay Leno, was there when David opened. This was in 1975. Leno was watching the tryouts as he did every evening, as it was his habit to do. He was always on the lookout for good new comedians with new slants on old material and new insights into the craft of comedy that he might be able to incorporate for himself.

Then suddenly there was this guy—Leno found out later that he was from Indiana—who pulled up in the parking lot in a pickup truck. To Leno the only thing that was *wrong* was the fact that he had a sixties beard and that he really resembled Dinty Moore in the *Bringing up Father* cartoon strip.

Leno said later he was entranced by the soft, persuasive voice of Letterman. And then the import of the material sank in. The man was *funny*. Leno tried to remember what Letterman had said. Something like this: "We are diametrically opposed to the use of orphans as yardage markers on driving ranges."

It was funny! The man was an original. He was so much more advanced than the others that he stood out. His delivery was quiet, controlled—impeccable. He was cool and savvy. His material was sophisticated, intellectually superior, and subtly memorable.

About Leno's comedy, Letterman thought: "Aw, see, *that's* how it's supposed to be done!" It wasn't bathroom humor, it wasn't a couple of guys going into a bar. It was smart, sociologically hip observation. It could be on any level—politics, television, education. "The dynamic of it was, you and I both understand that this is stupid. We're Jay's hip friends."

To Dave's surprise, Leno introduced himself to Letterman. "Gee!" Leno said. "You got great stuff."

Letterman said of Leno: "His attitude was so clearly defined, and he was so bright and so contemporary and he did it so effortlessly, it just seemed like an extension of his personality. And that really crystallized for me what I wanted to do."

And he went on. "[Leno] was head and shoulders above anybody else. I patterned much of what I did on what I saw him do. It's no surprise to any of us that he's gotten so successful. I think everybody was surprised that it took him a little longer. The first night I saw him, I thought the next day he was going to be a huge star."

What Letterman really borrowed from Jay Leno was his technique for getting his humor across. What Dave supplied was his own inimitable point of view.

"I suppose I'm an observational comic. I try to serve my own sense of humor, and if other people like it, fine. What I look for are the setups in life, and then I fill in the punch lines. Like one of my favorite jokes came right out of the *National Enquirer,* which every week gives you a million setups. I'm standing there buying cantaloupes, and there's this headline in the *Enquirer* that says, 'How to Lose Weight without Diet or Exercise.' So I think to myself, 'That leaves disease.' I've been doing that [joke] word for word for years, and it never fails to get laughs."

The Comedy Store knew a good thing when it saw Letterman. He was hired to be one of their regulars—actually to receive pay to tell jokes. And then Jimmie Walker, at that time starring in the sitcom *Good Times* as "J.J.," hired him to write fifteen jokes a week for a hundred and fifty dollars.

"He wanted me to write jokes with a black point of view," Dave recalled. "He was the first black person I had ever seen."

Once Jack Rollins got working for him in 1977, Letterman found better gigs. One that was especially intriguing was the new *Mary Tyler Moore Show.* Somehow Rollins got a part in it for Letterman.

And just to prove that 1977 wasn't entirely a gap in the calendar of good things, it brought with it a woman named Merrill Markoe, who would prove to be a very important figure in David Letterman's future.

It was more or less a coincidence that Merrill got a job writing for the Moore show just at the time David was involved with it. She was able to help him over some of the worst hurdles—and hurdles there were aplenty.

Merrill was a writer, a graduate of the University of California at Berkeley. She wound up teaching art at the University of Southern California in Los Angeles. Suffering from boredom in her job, she tried working up a stand-up act on her own at the Comedy Store to showcase her comedic talent. And she and Dave began dating.

The problem with Dave and the Moore show was the fact that he was cast as a buffoon—a clown—and it simply did not work since he had to dress up funny.

"I was just mortified," David confessed. "I was like a spring that was coiling ever more tightly."

He said later, when the show folded after only three weeks on the air, "It was pretty exciting, having heard about Television City all my life, to be going to work there. I had a name badge with a picture on it and an ID number, and I could eat in the CBS commissary. I could talk to Mary Tyler Moore anytime I wanted. I could do almost anything. I could share fruit with her if I wanted to. I, of course, wanted to. She never wanted any part of it.

"But the hard part was that I had to sing and dance and dress up in costumes. That was tough. I knew my limitations, but this really brought them home [to me]. You know, it was, 'You're not a singer. You're not a dancer. You're not an actor. Get out of here. What are you doing? Get away from Mary. That's her fruit. Don't try and eat that fruit.' "

Nevertheless his appearance on the ill-fated show brought him to the attention of Johnny Carson's staff, and on November 26, 1978, a month and a half after the Moore show died, David Letterman was sitting down and talking to Johnny Carson on *The Tonight Show*.

After that, spots appeared regularly here and there. He was a panelist on *The Gong Show*, a celebrity contestant for a week on *The Twenty Thousand Dollar Pyramid*, hosted by Dick Clark, and an actor on *Mork and Mindy*. Then he was on *The Liar's Club* as a "celebrity"—which Letterman called a "source of amusement" to him.

And then in April 1979, NBC offered Letterman a two-year contract, with no specific show mentioned. Later, the show turned out to be tentatively titled *Leave It to Dave*.

"The whole project was just a disaster from Word One. I was supposed to sit on a throne, and the set was all pyramids. The walls were all covered in shag carpet. It was like some odd Egyptian theme sale at Carpenteria.

"At one point I was in New York and I got a phone call from the West Coast. They said, 'We've come up with a great idea. Your guests will all sit around on pillows.' And I hung up the phone and I turned to my manager, Jack Rollins, and I said, 'This moron wants us to sit on pillows. What's the matter with chairs?' You could just see the elements kind of—I hate to say it was like dominoes toppling, but it was like dominoes toppling."

At that point Fred Silverman stepped in with a morning talk show for Dave, to be broadcast from New York, with the format more or less left up to Dave. His first move was to hire Merrill as his head writer. He then hired Bob Stewart, an experienced producer. Unfortunately, Stewart was a producer of *game shows*. There was tension on the set. Four days before the show was to open, Stewart left the program, at Dave's request.

The *New York Post*'s "Page Six" led off with these words: "In an astonishing high-level shake-up, the top two producers of the *David Letterman Show* have resigned, only days before this morning's scheduled debut of the NBC talk show. . . . Letterman's daily ninety-minute live program is a pet project of his mentor Fred Silverman. The shake-up seems to indicate yet more trouble in the NBC studios—as well as Letterman's clout. Nobody will say what caused the turmoil, but insiders believe it had to do with the format."

Merrill agreed to step into the spot vacated by the producers.

"The show was running us," said David. "Actually, it was

chasing us down the street. But NBC told us not to worry. They said, 'You have twenty-six weeks. Let it evolve."

Letterman's main problem was how to fill ninety minutes with comedy and laughs. "I would throw little fits when they'd say, 'We want you to have a psychic on,' and I'd say, 'No, I don't want to have a psychic on.' And they'd say, 'Well, try it,' and we'd try it, and it would just be awful and embarrassing. I didn't know really how you had a discussion on a topic like that with a network executive. My forte was not personnel. I didn't realize that politically what you have to do is to say, 'Fine, we'll be happy to,' and then forget it. You forget all about it. And then six months later, they say, 'Did we have a psychic on?' and you say, 'Yeah, well, the plane got stuck in Alabama, they couldn't get here.' "

But even planned things turned into immediate disasters. As a gag, the director let a tiny herd of sheep into the studio. The sheep began pushing their way through the chairs and desks until it was bedlam. No one could control them.

Letterman's face lit up like a lamp. It was a moment of unmitigated disaster. Yet somehow it was something that was right up Letterman's alley. He positively glowed with excitement.

In his most cutting and sarcastic tone he tried to snatch victory from the jaws of defeat by pretending everything was all right. But the sarcasm and irony was overridden by a thoroughly amused and civilized persona within him that looked at the world in a very special way—the Letterman way.

"Ladies and gentlemen, what you are witnessing here is a good idea gone awry. Yes, a fun-filled surprise turning into an incredible screwup."

Somehow, in this final moment of total catastrophe, Letterman was up to his ears in chaos. And yet, floundering there, he was able somehow to resurface uninjured. He had found his voice. And the voice, the decent voice of reason and logic, turned the shambles into a bizarre pattern of peace and harmony.

Nevertheless, that fact did not save the show. It was doomed. Even the news never came over right. Edwin Newman read several five-minute newscasts between the show segments. But it was not your usual news features. It wasn't the *news* that was unusual; it was the *audience.*

"Ed was doing the news for the first time in front of a live audience. They would cheer at stories they liked, and hiss and boo at ones they didn't. It was like doing the news in a nightclub, and Ed really rolled with the punches. He learned to pace himself to keep up with the audience."

The show never did get rolling. After its initial broadcast on June 23, 1980, there were only about three months of actual scheduling.

When the show was finally canceled in September, Letterman said, "It was the best and the worst experience of my life. I was on a plane back to California, and I was thinking, 'Now what do I do?' "

Merrill said, "He was pretty sure he would never work again. He's a pessimist, and this gave him a chance to be *really* pessimistic."

Letterman: "It was like falling down an endless shaft into the miasma."

Merrill: "The morning show was a delusion in the sense that we felt you could just do whatever comedy you wanted, any time of day or night. And when the show started to fail, Dave was going crazy. It was not a happy time."

It was Letterman who saw the show for what it was with unusual clarity of vision and understanding.

"Every day was a fistfight," he said of the disaster. "The first director was a game-show director, and he could direct a game show in his sleep, but he couldn't direct a talk show. Basic rules of television directing were being violated left and right.

"The guest would be saying something and the light would be on me. I'd be asking and the shot would be on who knows what. Finally he started to shoot everything with one wide shot. It looked like a security camera at 7-Eleven.

"I mean, it just stunk. The ratings weren't going up, and then we had a meeting with the NBC executive in charge of the show."

She was quite laid back about the chaos around her. "Well, you've just got to work harder," she told all of them.

And then, as Letterman put it, "She left for a four-day weekend in Maine."

Letterman remembered screaming at her: "What do you mean, *work harder?* It's like we've been holding *back* here? Like we know we've got a spot in the playoffs, and now we'll really turn it on?"

Letterman shook his head at the memory. "Finally, we lost four Group W stations—Boston, Philadelphia, San Francisco, and Detroit—in one fell swoop. There was a piece in the *Los Angeles Times* about the disaster that was daytime television, thanks to us, and it mentioned that the Westinghouse stations had pulled out and the affiliates were grumbling. That's how I found out about it. So it was from that point on that we said, 'Screw it, we've got nothing to lose. We're sinking. Let's do whatever we want to do.' "

And they did exactly that.

CHAPTER FIVE
Breaking Through

The deep gloom that had at first settled on David Letterman at the cancellation of his morning show soon was dissipated in the warm, bright sunshine of southern California. He finally accepted the fact that he had flopped at what he thought he did best.

And then, looking back on it, he realized that what he had been doing was good. It was right in line with what he thought comedy should be. His experiments had usually been on target. Somehow the time slot might have been wrong. Perhaps . . .

Actually, with contract money coming in, being out of work in California wasn't all that terrible for Letterman. He spent time playing a little racquetball, dropping in on his friends, and fooling around with his German shepherds. The leisure was great—but there was so much of it!

Salvation came for him not in 1981, his year-long exile from the communications industry, but in 1982, and it came, indirectly of course, in the unlikely form of a television film commentator named Rona Barrett.

Barrett had been assigned to cohost a ninety-minute show called *Tomorrow: Coast to Coast*. Tom Snyder had been the host of *The Tomorrow Show*, a one-hour show broadcast between 1 and 2 A.M. on NBC. When Johnny Carson's ninety-minute show was reduced to sixty minutes, the NBC brass added a half hour to Snyder's show and changed its title and pitch.

Snyder's show had been a hard-news interview show featuring real newsmakers in the style of Ted Koppel's *Nightline* later on.

Snyder was a somewhat brash newsman who had wooed and won an audience of college students who liked him because he asked the celebrities and movers and shakers tough questions that sometimes embarrassed them. By expanding the show, NBC thought it should lighten the load on Snyder and let Barrett shoulder it with show-biz fluff.

When the change occurred, Snyder's fans hated Barrett and said so. The new viewers who were into entertainment hated Snyder's straight stuff and sometimes wild interviews. But the hostility was not confined to the viewing audience. There were numerous fights on air between Barrett and Snyder. Finally, Barrett walked out. NBC filled in the gaps with up-and-coming stand-up comics.

The ratings sank through the floor.

On November 10, 1981, the show was yanked. Snyder was out. Programming called in David Letterman. The plan was to substitute a new version of the *David Letterman Show*— this one sixty minutes long—to begin after the Carson show ended. Carson endorsed Letterman and agreed that his production company would coproduce the Letterman show.

This was great news for David. "We knew what we wanted to do and whom we wanted to do it with. We brought Barry Sand back as producer . . . and Merrill as head writer, and Hal Gurnee, a wonderful and extremely creative guy who, incidentally, used to be Jack Paar's director, to direct. We hired a small staff of bright, funny, sensitive people who never want to go to the Polo Lounge for Perrier."

On February 1, 1982, *Late Night with David Letterman* premiered on NBC at 12:30 A.M. with a show that was hoped would knock the socks off the new viewers. Letterman's attitude was somewhat different as he noted: "Well, let's just try not to embarrass ourselves unnecessarily."

The first on the bill was a group of six chorus girls running around in circles and flailing the air with colored feathers. These were the Rainbow Grill Peacock Girls, according to the announcement. "You know spring is just around the corner when the Peacock Girls begin to molt."

In some ways, David Letterman's genius was in parodying the very medium in which he operated: that is, television. The Peacock Girls were modified—comedified—versions of the Rockettes of Rockefeller Center, or the Can Can girls of Paris. They were archetypal examples of old-fashioned show business itself—high kicking, high stepping, and high riding. Dancing girls would become a kind of set feature on *Late Night* now and again, just to keep things in focus and remind the viewers of exactly who was being kidded.

Suddenly, there was David Letterman in jeans and jacket announcing that he would be taking the audience on a tour of the set. In the control room the staff, dressed in Bavarian peasant costumes, were drinking and singing lewd songs. The Green Room was indeed green—with flowering shrubs, plants, and trees imploding on the dressing room.

"These are some of the very few vegetables here at NBC not in programming," Letterman noted happily

In parodying television, Letterman always knew that he could find plenty of things in his very own show to laugh about. The walking tour of the set would become another staple of *Late Night*. It would come in many guises: interviews with members of the audience; prowls through backstage; peeks into the workings of the control room. And there would always be good mileage in kidding the television Establishment itself.

The first celebrity guest on the opener was Bill Murray. He told David he had an urge to sing "Let's Get Physical" and do some aerobics. The act was very funny.

Actually, the story *behind* the act was even funnier. Murray had been invited to Letterman's office to discuss things with the writers on the show to come up with something. On the morning he arrived, Merrill and David were out shooting a remote. Murray brought a half-dozen bottles of tequila with him, at which point he and the entire staff of writers proceeded to get—as Letterman described it later—"shit-faced" drunk.

The place was a shambles when Letterman returned, and everyone was reeling. Murray had convinced the writers that the fluorescent lights in the lamps were draining their vitamin E—they were hidden away out of sight. Of course, nothing had been written for Murray.

Letterman: "The only explanation I could get out of anyone was [a cryptic] 'Bill was here.' "

So much for careful research and agonizing preparation.

Letterman had always been an easy mark for a comic who wanted to do his own thing to the nth degree. The madness of Bill Murray's actions were typical of that kind of crazy activity. In a way, madness was better when it was totally unpredictable—that is, unprepared. It, too, would become a staple on *Late Night*'s madness.

Following Murray's act was the remote that Letterman had been out filming, titled "Shame of the City." The idea was to see New York as it was, including its *shame*.

And David found it. It was a sign in a window of a delicatessen: "Planing a party? Try one of theese." The dialogue consisted of Letterman berating the deli owner for misspelling "planing" and "theese" and refusing to leave until the man promised to fix the sign.

Letterman, dourly: "Truly a shame of the city!" Then he brightened up. "Another blight remedied—and I'm proud to be part of it!"

From the beginning of the morning show that had failed, Letterman loved to prowl the streets of the big city for material that was real—and funny at the same time. The remotes would become a main feature of *Late Night*. This was where David Letterman could use his comedic talents in interviewing real people—not celebrities—to the utmost, getting himself down to the level of the public and the people who really made the city run. The butcher. The baker. The pizza man. The deli operator.

At one point the show's host said, "The fact that we're on at 12:30 at night by definition ought to create an air of excitement. Of course, that's an illusion—it's only television. We're not changing history—though we've got that scheduled for the second night."

At another point he said, "I'm accustomed to small audiences. There's a joke around here—my old show was on when everybody is at work, and this one's on when everybody's asleep."

And finally, "I *like* being back in New York City. We can roll a television camera onto Sixth Avenue, and it will be stolen in a matter of minutes."

New York was always the perfect target for Letterman's zany wit. He would continue to attack the great city's foibles night after night in his lead-in remarks. He was now operating at the perfect time to allow the city to see itself as it really was—and laugh a little at the boldness and the badness exposed without mercy by Letterman's prowling mind and his irrepressible wit.

Now Letterman was finding that what he had thought about when he was doing his other show was true. His other morning show had been canceled before its time. In fact, it had been a perfect proving ground for material that would work. And, of course, it was a fact that it would work better in the wee small *early*-morning hours.

The reviews of the show were generally kind, although there were some vicious swipes here and there that would serve as a warning to David Letterman to work on his *attitude*, since in that area he might be somewhat vulnerable.

Variety, the voice of the entertainment business, was rough on the show—much rougher than usual for a television presentation. Its reviewer hated the monologue. Hated the star's delivery. Hated the humor, categorizing it "feeble." Hated the Bill Murray-David Letterman dialogue, likening it to a duel between two comics who had no sense of comedy. Hated Letterman's presence, observing that he was "visibly uncomfortable."

And yet in the end the review noted: "But with his casual, unpredictable sense of humor, Letterman is an amusing man. His low-key, slightly off-kilter way of looking at things seems well suited to a late-night time slot."

James Wolcott described Letterman in the *Village Voice*:

"Like Johnny Carson, David Letterman is a comic with droll timing, flip-top wit, and a sure sense of how far he can push a suggestive joke without offending the sensibilities of the more conservative sleepy-pies out there in the great American heartland."

Letterman was not, however, the kind of star who enjoyed "swinging from the chandelier." "He's more of a sneak wise-cracker, flipping off funny quick comments like a pitcher with a deft pick-off move."

Wolcott ended the piece: "I really do enjoy David Letterman's understated style and sorely want the show to succeed."

The *New York Post* gave the show an A-minus grade. "If this is a hip generation's Carson show, Letterman hasn't done it off the cuff. His taped bits like 'Shame of the City' were cheeky and fine. Letterman works hard without showing the sweat. Get thee behind me, Don Rickles."

TV Guide's Robert MacKenzie said, "Letterman is trim, smirky, quick-witted, and cocky. Like him or not, he is one of the more interesting talents to come along in a decade." But, MacKenzie went on, he was a "rotten interviewer." The reason for saying that? "A man who mocks everyone and everything can be amusing in spurts but wearing in the long haul."

The *New York Times* was quite charitable. Tony Schwartz wrote: "While Mr. Letterman's first effort was uneven, it seems fair to assume that the show will need time to hit its stride. Mr. Letterman's style is low-key and laid back . . . and so he is more of an acquired taste than most comedians." Schwartz hoped he would relax into the "loopy informality" that made him "so whimsically and unpredictably appealing" in his canceled A.M. show.

More importantly, the Nielsens were good. *Late Night* got a 2.7 rating and a 14 share, both very good numbers for the late-night audience. Letterman was pulling in about twice the viewers Tom Snyder got in the same slot. About half of them were in that coveted eighteen to thirty-four age range—the so-called trend-setting and high-disposable-income group.

The show continued on in its unique shambling gait. In the

days and weeks that followed, the jokes continued in the same light laid-back vein:

"You folks are easily entertained," Letterman said one night, "and boy, did you come to the right place!"

Later he cautioned his viewers: "Keep reminding yourself, 'Yes, this is actually network television.' "

Even the announcer, Bill Wendell, got to make use of the Letterman humor as he introduced his host:

"And now, a man who is frightened by the slightest change in air temperature—David Letterman!"

With a wackier and more sophisticated slant later in the week: "And now, a man who once saw Maurice Evans in a restaurant—David Letterman!"

One night Letterman said that he had accidentally left his "artificial tooth" at home. That bit obviously came from his conversation with *The Peeping Times* girl who wanted him to have the gap between his two front teeth capped. A housewife in the audience—she was from New York State—was recruited by the announcer from the audience to host the show for a few minutes.

Later on when the show had gained its momentum as the craziest thing in town, one whole evening was shown entirely from David Letterman's point of view. A hand-held camera allowed viewers to see everything on the set from the host's point of view. The cue card could be seen plainly in front of the camera. On the cue card were the words, "Burt, the Human Caboose." Suddenly, that card was replaced by another that said, "Dump the Caboose!"

At the same moment Letterman was heard to say, "Darn the luck, Burt, we're out of time!"

In July 1982, *Late Night with David Letterman* came up with a first. They offered their Christmas special six months early—"to beat the rush."

And sure enough, one night a new "Stupid Pet Trick" appeared, when a white rabbit named Thumper rode a skateboard across the show's set. Actually, the stupid pet trick was the invention of Merrill Markoe, and it had been proved out on the morning show that had flopped.

Just to show that incongruous wackiness had no limits, Letterman brought out a certain Dr. Norman Hoffman for an interview titled "Limited Perspective." It was to be a dentist's view of the motion picture *Reds*.

In a serious vein, Dr. Hoffman said that in the film, which took place during World War I when the czar was overthrown and Communism became the government of the Russian people, he thought that the actors' teeth were not convincing as pre-Revolutionary dentures.

Letterman nodded profoundly. "Pretty much ruined the film for you, huh?"

The near-misses were sometimes the best bits. When a celebrity guest was late one night, Letterman got the producer of the segment, and a writer on the show named Gerard Mulligan, to help out.

"What do you think the guest would say if he were here tonight?" he asked with a straight face.

Mulligan was game, and went right at it. His ad lib speech was full of non sequiturs, imaginative turns, and some double talk.

A staff member informed Letterman that the absent guest's manager was backstage. Letterman had him come out. The manager refused, and so all of them trooped into the Green Room and talked first to the manager and then other guests who were waiting to go on.

It was bizarre, odd ball, and fantastically funny.

"I love stuff like that," David said later. "When something collapses, it's fun to see what I can build out of the wreckage." He was recalling the sheep episode on the morning show when he had seen the possibilities of what he could do when the situation seemed irretrievable.

Most of the reviews that followed the opener show were favorable, although some carped on Letterman's space-age humor. Within weeks, however, NBC found that the people who watched Letterman were loyal fans who talked about the show to everyone they knew.

"This is the Number One college show in the country," John Maas, director of East Coast programming, told reporters. They took it all down dutifully. "It's a cult already. People talk and say, 'Did you see what they did last night on Letterman?' I mean they *really* love him."

Cult?

David Letterman shuddered when he read the word in the paper. "Cult brings to mind a curious kind of people living in tents outside of Barstow. Privately, I think that I'm not really somebody who has a network television show. Celebrities are other people—Johnny Carson and Sylvester Stallone. I'm just a kid trying to make a living is the way I feel.

"Here I am, waiting for the fat kid to put unleaded gas in my car, and I'm asking him if I can do it because he's having trouble resetting the pump, and I think, 'I'm not really that person on television.' It always surprises me that what I do in New York between 5:30 and 6:30 P.M. [the time of the taping] will show up later that night in Albuquerque and Seattle.

"It's like tossing a rock into a pond and watching the ripples cross the water. I don't like to think about it—it's a little more responsibility than a guy would want."

Getting away from the idea of being a cult figure, Letterman pointed out that he was concerned about tomorrow rather than today.

"What I'd like is for this show to stay on long enough to become just a pattern of American television. If we're still on the air in five years, then I'll think of it as a success."

He then cited the reason he thought that Johnny Carson was still on the air after twenty-odd years.

"It's not because he does a *great* show every night. He has his great shows, and he has his awful shows, like everybody else. But the reason the *Tonight Show* succeeds is because people like *him*. They don't really turn the show on to see whoever Johnny has as guests. They turn on the show to see Johnny."

As for Letterman, "We're just trying to have a good time. There are places for thought-provoking material, but not on our show. Maybe *Nightline*. It's really frivolous. It's a silly show. And by design."

CHAPTER SIX
Late-Night Laughs

It did not take long for *Late Night with David Letterman* to begin to catch on with a rather eclectic crowd of college kids, insomniac adults, sophisticates of all ages, "in" people, and a handful of movers and shakers. The show did have a format, but somehow it was just a bit off.

There was no telling when host David Letterman might decide *not* to do the show and leave it in the entirely inept hands of someone not even remotely connected with the entertainment business. Or he might trick up the camera work.

One of the most outrageous gimmicks he ever pulled was the "360 degree" broadcast, in which the picture on the home set made one complete rotation in the hour the show was on. Halfway through, at 1 A.M., Letterman and his guest actually appeared upside down on the viewer's set.

In another runaway camera ploy, Letterman's camera crew strapped a minicam on the back of a chimpanzee that was then set loose to run rampant through the studio.

Letterman refused adamantly to have an Ed McMahon on his show—someone he could talk to and who would laugh uproariously at his jokes. Instead, he would find himself chatting somewhat aimlessly with his spaced-out band leader, Paul Shaffer, who led the World's Most Dangerous Band.

And, later on, he added another professional nerd to perform idiotic chores for him. This man was an actor named Calvert DeForest who became known on the show as Larry "Bud" Melman. One of Melman's first appearances was at the Soviet Consulate in New York, where he could be seen distributing pamphlets urging defection to Soviet tourists and offering American appliances and pornography to citizens in exchange for betraying their country.

Another time Melman appeared at the main bus terminal in mid-Manhattan, handing out hot towels to the exhausted and sweating passengers debarking from the buses.

Except for those who understood what Letterman was trying to do, most of the viewers were puzzled at these antics.

There were also skits put on by a group of actors—some of them were the writers on the show—that kidded the mores of Americans, especially New Yorkers. Writers like Chris Elliott (the son of Bob Elliott of the famous Bob and Ray radio team), Gerard Mulligan, Larry Jacobson, and Steve O'Donnell (head writer).

The *New York Times* rather accurately called the Letterman show "an absurdist parody of mass culture"—but in spite of the fact that it went over the heads of many viewers who just didn't get it, it became solidly established in the late-night firmament.

Although its success was an unbelievable development to many knowledgeable executives in the television industry, there was one good reason why the show began to catch on. That one reason was the instinctive and well-honed wit of its star, David Letterman.

Although his so-called stand-up routine at the beginning of the show was not actually in the style of Johnny Carson's opener, Letterman's comments were hewed expertly to his own modus operandi in delivering a joke.

An analysis of the Letterman MO is difficult, but it has a lot to do *not* with the words in which the joke idea is verbalized, but in the *way* in which it is delivered to the audience.

This is in no way saying that Letterman uses exaggerated body language in the manner of Jay Leno, who can make anybody laugh with some of his facial and body contortions. With Letterman, the distortion is in the inflection of the voice, in perhaps a twinkle of the eye, or maybe in the slight grimace—almost subliminal—that precedes or follows the key phrase of the joke.

Generally his jokes tended to be imitations of his youthful pranks in Broad Ripple, Indiana. He loved still to con unwary people into special traps:

"Tourists—have some fun with New York's hard-boiled cabbies. When you get to your destination, say to your driver, 'Pay? I was hitchhiking.'"

But he also borrowed heavily from the huge pool of laugh-provoking names that circulated continuously in political and celebrity circles. As for example:

"Hal Mason died in Los Angeles yesterday at the age of sixty-nine. He was the creator of such delightful cartoon characters as the Pillsbury Dough Boy, Mr. Clean, and Ed Meese."

He never let up on lampooning the straight-arrow credibility of tourists gawking at the high buildings in New York:

"Tip to out-of-town visitors: If you buy something here in New York and want to have it shipped home, be suspicious if the clerk tells you they don't need your name and address."

But he was equally hard on the well-heeled sports entrepreneurs, as he reported once when the brand-new United States Football League (now defunct) filed an antitrust lawsuit against the National Football League in Federal District Court in New York:

"There were 150 people in the courtroom—third-largest crowd ever to see the USFL in action."

And he was always ready to give a backhanded compliment to New York City:

"According to the new *Rand-McNally Places-Rated Almanac*, the best place to live in America is the city of Pittsburgh. The city of New York came in twenty-fifth. Here in New York we really don't care too much. Because we know that we could beat up their city anytime."

He retained his collegiate sense of the absurdity of stating the obvious, as in this report of a newspaper clipping:

"A poll in *USA Today* said that three out of four people in this country make up 75 percent of the population."

For the sophisticated New Yorker, totally loyal to this giant metropolis yet brutally aware of its deficiencies, he had this local scene to report:

"Today at lunchtime in midtown, a group of stunned New Yorkers stood on the sidewalk with their mouths open, pointing at something that obviously paralyzed them with amazement. Finally, a tourist from Boston came along and explained that it was a parking space."

Moving out of New York City and onto the national scene, he used another great name from that pool of laugh-provokers, and came up with:

"The commissioners of the NFL and the NBA met with Nancy Reagan yesterday to discuss the drug problem. Asked what the First Lady said, NBA Commissioner David Stern replied, 'She asked me if I'd ever seen Magic Johnson naked.' "

And then he took a pot shot at the medical fraternity:

"This warning from the New York City Department of Health Fraud: Be suspicious of any doctor who tries to take your temperature with his finger."

The New York scene seemed almost always foremost in his mind:

"Someone did a study on the three most-often-heard phrases in New York City. One is, 'Hey, taxi!' Two is, 'What train do I take to get to Bloomingdale's?' And three is, 'Don't worry. It's just a flesh wound.' "

And so was the violence and mayhem never far off in Manhattan:

"Every year when it's Chinese New Year here in New York, there are fireworks going off at all hours. New York mothers calm their frightened children by telling them it's just gunfire."

Occasionally he made a comment of one kind or another about the international scene, as this one during the Lebanon troubles:

"In Lebanon, switching to Daylight Saving Time is causing

a problem, because they have to turn back all the time bombs an hour."

Then he might return to one of the big names to combine two incongruous lines of thought in this fashion:

"On Nancy Reagan's recent birthday, she said she was fifty-nine, although records reportedly showed she was sixty-one. Her explanation: she doesn't count the two years she spent in the National Hockey League."

To cap it all off with a typical absurdity that had become grist for the mill in his humor for years:

"I saw something in the paper the other day that's a good example of what they mean by federal waste: A professor of pharmacology at Penn State just got a grant of $150,000 from the U.S. Public Health Service to develop a time-release placebo."

For a change of pace, the staff of *Late Night* invented a special humor format for Letterman. This one was called the "Myth or Fact?" joke. The idea was to verbalize a myth, and then deflate it with factual material that could prove it no more than a chimera. Of course, the joke depended on what the myth entailed:

"MYTH: 'Hal Gurnee'—listed in the show's credits as 'director'—does not exist. It is really just a name owned by NBC, and no more refers to a real person than 'Betty Crocker' or 'Aunt Jemima' do. As an economy measure, the show has no director, and the listing of 'Hal Gurnee' represents a compromise the network worked out with the Director's Guild.

"FACT: Hal Gurnee is a respected director of the kind of television represented by *Late Show*. (Incidentally, similar stories have circulated about Johnny Carson, Merv Griffin, and Diane Sawyer.)"

Another special humor format that Letterman came up with was called "Viewer Mail." The answers given by Letterman might be humorous, deadpan, or simply a straight answer.

"Blue Hill, ME. Oct. 27th. Dear Mr. Letterman. How come we never see it raining or snowing outside your window? I can hardly believe that it never rains or snows in New York City. . . . The last time I was in New York City, I couldn't get one wink of sleep on account of the noise on the streets. But there is no noise coming from outside your window. How come? Larry W."

"Larry, you were probably in New York a couple of years ago—about the time when there was all that construction noise when they were building the giant climate-dome. . . . Well, the mammoth plastic-and-steel bubble has been in place for quite a while now—and every day here in New York City it's a balmy sixty-eight degrees. No rain, no snow."

One night Letterman presented a tongue-in-cheek essay on television concerning the right and wrong way to act as a guest on the show. The rules were presented as "Talk Show Etiquette":

"Booking guests on a show such as *Late Night* is a difficult and time-consuming task. Sooner or later, just about everyone will be called upon to be a talk-show guest. In the event that you do become a guest on our show, your interview will be a lot more pleasant if you take the time to learn the accepted rules of talk-show etiquette.

"Rule #1. No beach attire. No shirt, no shoes—no interview.

"Rule #2. Know who and where your host is. Every guest receives a photo of the host . . . and a map of where to find him [on the set]. If you get lost, use them.

"Rule #3. Take off your Walkman. If you're booked as a guest on this show, at least *pretend* to be interested. When you walk onto the set, the host will shake your hand. It is customary to take advantage of this opportunity to slip the host a hundred [dollars]. He will like you better and ask nicer questions.

"Rule #4. Even if they assure you that they'll just watch quietly and won't be any trouble, *don't bring your parents.* Sorry, but it's our show policy.

"Rule #5. The phone is here for *my* use only. No personal calls during the show.

"Rule #6. When your interview is over, just go quietly. When I say, 'Thank you very much. Come back any time," what I *mean* is, take a *hike.*

"Lastly, if you're booked as a guest, try not to die on the

show. A dead guest is a dull guest. It puts a damper on proceedings. And there might be a comedian following you."

There were a lot of visual gags, too. One night the staff came up with an enormous doorknob and handed it to Letterman. He stared at it a long time, apparently in deep thought. Then he began musing aloud:

"This doorknob is really large. It's much bigger than it ought to be. It's *just plain big.* I don't know. Maybe every generation reinvents the wheel for itself. Or the Giant Doorknob."

Among the more complicated action gags that were perpetrated on the *Late Show* was a blockbuster that absolutely riveted the audience to the set. With some concern, Letterman announced that he wanted to know what it felt like to be a potato chip lowered into a plate of onion dip. And so he said he decided to have himself converted into a giant potato chip to be lowered into one ton of onion dip.

And the staff covered him with potato chips until he could hardly be seen and lowered him into a vat of dip.

Later, he was asked how it felt to be a potato chip, and if he wasn't embarrassed by the routine.

"I *did* mind doing it. I have a real low threshold of embarrassment. It may be hard to tell that I'm easily embarrassed from watching the show. Or it may be that I'm in the wrong line of work. But that sort of thing pierces the flatness of the television screen.

"It's great if you can get people to actually *talk* about something they saw on television. In the first years of television, that's all people did talk about, because there never had been television before. But now, heavens, we've just seen it all."

Another gag involved Tom Selleck, a guest on the show. Somehow Letterman conned him into sticking his head in a tub of water to perform imitations of a motorboat in action.

At another time he persuaded Mariel Hemingway to show him how to clean fish preparatory to cooking.

But it was with Don King that Letterman almost accidentally discovered one of his most underrated talents.

King, a well-known sports promoter, did, and still does,

comb his hair into the most outrageous do anyone ever saw—especially for a male. The strands of hair stand up on end as if electrified in the manner of Elsa Lanchester's locks while she was turning into the Bride of Frankenstein.

For a long time Letterman stared at King's hair and then he leaned slightly forward and lowered his voice:

"Let me ask you something: What's the deal with your hair?"

What Letterman and his viewers discovered at that moment was the startling fact that even if Letterman *did* ask a tasteless question, he did not openly offend his guest or his viewers. Except on various occasions—some of which are discussed later on in this book. In effect, it opened up Letterman's concept of an interview and led to a number of interesting variations and questions later on in the life of the show.

Of course, the Stupid Pet Tricks, carried over from the *Leave It to Dave* morning show continued to be a big hit on *Late Night*. In one instance, a dog showed that he had learned how to play basketball. In another, a dog had been trained to carry money to a package store and return with a six-pack of beer.

Most comedians hired professional comics to warm up their audiences for them. Letterman was not of that particular mind-set. He did his own.

"What a night!" he said once. "Can you feel the electricity in the air? Can you feel the excitement? Well, then, you're in the wrong place!" A pause. "Aw, come on folks—it was a *joke*. How much time we got? Thirty seconds? I got to go. 'Bye! Enjoy the show."

And he was out of there.

Letterman once claimed that his show thrived on a special kind of thing. He called it "found comedy," and then tried to describe that type of humor in detail.

"We do a lot of what we call 'found comedy,' things you find in newspapers. [And in] viewer mail. The fact that January actually *is* National Soup Month, so we're saluting soup all this month. I don't know if this stuff is more funny, but I do know that I feel more comfortable dealing with something

For some reason, Letterman always liked to play the tough guy as an act. In September 1991 he was beginning to feud with NBC. Take that, Peacock! (FRANK W. OCKENFELS III/ OUTLINE)

Early days with David
Letterman on the NBC
Late Night show. Note
longer hair from a
younger America.
(NBC/GLOBE PHOTOS)

One of the latest
pictures of David
Letterman on his
CBS *Late Show*.
Note nattier suit
and shorter haircut.
(PHOTOFEST)

David Letterman guests on John Carson's *Tonight Show*, with its familiar background of Los Angeles at night. (SUZIE BLEEDEN/GLOBE PHOTOS)

Johnny Carson visits David Letterman on *Late Night* and cracks up his host with a telephone conversation purportedly to Letterman's mother. (EVERETT COLLECTION, INC.)

In 1979, with Letterman sitting in as guest host on the
Tonight Show, Jay Leno was guest. The two schmoozed
like old hands at the game, although neither of them had a
show then. (NBC/GLOBE PHOTOS)

Howard Stern was always a puzzle to David Letterman, who
could not believe, some times, the absolutely revolting things
that Stern was saying. (NBC/GLOBE PHOTOS)

Sonny Bono and Cher,
long after their divorce,
reunite to visit *Late
Night*, where the host
seems excluded from
the conversation.
(EVERETT COLLECTION,
INC.)

Bruce Willis, star of
TV's *Moonlighting*,
regales David
Letterman with a
bit of show biz
blarney. (EVERETT
COLLECTION, INC.)

David Letterman in his customary cigar-smoking form chatting with guest Gary Shandling, star of *It's Gary Shandling's Show*, an acclaimed sitcom of the late eighties. (STEVE GRANITZ/RETNA LTD.)

Here the *Late Night* host seems to be in another world from his guest, Michael J. Fox, star of the TV sitcom, *Family Ties*, a fact which seems to bother Fox very little. (BILL DAVILA/ RETNA LTD.)

David Letterman announces on January 14, 1993 that he is going to leave NBC for CBS to appear on the *Late Show*, opposite the *Tonight Show*, and can't help flashing a fourteen-million-dollar grin for the cameras. (MICHAEL HIRSCH/SYGMA)

Letterman clutches an Emmy presented to him in 1986 not for being a talk-show host but for "outstanding writing in a variety music program," specifically, the Fourth Anniversary Show, *Late Night with David Letterman*. (WALTER MCBRIDE/ RETNA LTD.)

At eighteen, David Letterman smiles for his high school yearbook. Activities listed include basketball, track, "Ripples" (a musical), hall monitor, and band. (COURTESY OF BROAD RIPPLE HIGH SCHOOL)

that's actually there than with some lame premise we cook up [out of nothing]."

And yet, even with all the effort put into it, a show could fail. Many nights were negatives. But many more succeeded than failed. What made one show fail was hard to determine. But Letterman thought he had the answer to what made it succeed or fail:

"*I* do. It's the truth. If a show sucks, it's me. I've mishandled it. Butchered it. Not been prepared. Not asked the right questions. Not thought of something funny to say. Flubbed a joke. Missed a cue. Run a segment too long. It's all me. These people work hard every day assembling the elements of the show, and then it rests completely in my hands."

CHAPTER SEVEN
Top Ten—and Other—Lists

The David Letterman joke on *Late Night* that scored high-est and in the end became the most noted, most quoted, and most widely touted of all his routines was the Top Ten List. This proved to be an effective, almost perfect format for an endless series of one-line comments on politics, current events, sociology, and even on life itself.

What was official about the list was the following:

1. There were always ten items on the list.

2. The list was always read backward, from Number Ten on down to Number One.

What was unofficial about the list was the fact that it was the perfect way for Letterman to attack a situation. The beauty of the Top Ten List was the fact that he had at least ten shots at a funny joke, rather than just one. Usually one of the ten proved to be good enough for a belly laugh.

The first Top Ten appeared on the otherwise uneventful night of September 18, 1985, after *Late Night* had been airing four nights a week for at least three and a half years. It was originally devised as a thing the show would be doing "for two or three weeks."

In fact, if it had not eventually become an irresistible force, it would have died on meeting the original immovable object that was audience reaction. It did not die. It lived. It became a breathing, vital element of the show.

In its original bow it did not look anything like a winner. If anything, it appeared to be a loser in two directions: first, it seemed to be a parody of the basic "on a scale of One to Ten" idea; second, it was silly and off-the-beam—nothing like the later manifestations that grew out of the peculiar versatility of the format.

Here is the original, in its rather seedy persona:

"Top Ten Things That Almost Rhyme with *Peas*"

10. Heats.
 9. Rice.
 8. Moss.
 7. Ties.
 6. Needs.
 5. Lens.
 4. Ice.
 3. Nurse.
 2. Leaks.
 1. Meats.

Not a very impressive start, certainly. Yet in the long run this misshapen and ugly little format proved to be something that the Letterman show *needed* to justify its own existence on the airwaves.

Even so, in spite of the popularity of the gag, the Top Ten title on January 29, 1986, was "Reasons to Stop Doing the Top Ten." But that was soon followed by "Reasons to Continue the Top Ten List." And everybody breathed a sigh of relief.

The Top Ten List afforded Letterman a chance to attack all different kinds of problems. And it even allowed him a few short takes on very topical events in the news.

For an example of an irreverent look at a topical situation, take the one entitled "Top Ten Excuses of the Exxon Tanker Captain," which celebrated in a negative way the grounding of the *Valdez* and the resultant spill of millions of gallons of crude.

"Top Ten Excuses of the Exxon Tanker Captain"

10. Was trying to scrape ice off reef for margarita.
9. Thought harbor was filled with the soft, fluffy kind of rocks.
8. Felt flourishing salmon population was getting a little cocky lately.
7. Wanted to impress Jodie Foster.
6. Kept drinking beer to wash away taste of cheap scotch.
5. First mate and I were having "tastes great/less filling" argument.
4. Swerving to avoid oncoming Eastern Airlines jet.
3. You really need a good nap after downing a pitcher of frozen daiquiris.
2. Hoping to dislodge any whales that might be trapped in ice.
1. Man, was I *'faced!*

Next to topicality, the most popular target was any much-talked-about celebrity. Few big names could avoid staying off the Top Ten List. For example, here are three of "Princess Diana's Top Ten Complaints about Prince Charles":

8. Giggles like a schoolgirl around Buckingham Palace guards.
7. That phony British accent.
6. Never puts the cap back on the mango love butter.

But once the Top Ten was up to speed, many of the Lists contained pointed political statements. For example, even before the Nicaraguan Contra connection to the Iranian arms money was revealed, Letterman had a list. Here are four of his "Top Ten Explanations for the Iranian Arms Deal":

8. Disappointing profits from pro-Contra car wash.
5. Reagan heard Iraqi morning deejays make a lot of Nancy jokes.
3. President disoriented after day-long cough syrup party.
1. Idea of giving missiles to hostile nation looked good on paper.

Or take this one making fun of President Reagan's so-called inability to remember things:

"Top Ten Things Reagan *Does* Remember"

10. He used to live in a big, white house.
9. That bastard Sam Donaldson.
8. Those great parties at Marion Barry's.
7. Daughter Maureen's weight (within 150 lbs).
6. Where Nancy doesn't like to be touched.
5. The name, address, and Social Security number of each and every one of his black supporters.
4. If you need a hooker, call Bill Holden.
3. 4:30—Time for Wapner!
2. That Jodie Foster is a real troublemaker.
1. Falling off a horse, and that's about it.

Among celebrities, sports figures constantly found themselves targeted. Here are four of the "Top Ten Reasons Not to Suspend Pete Rose from Baseball":

10. Really young gamblers need a role model.
8. If suspended, might reveal identity of San Diego Chicken.
3. Baseball needs that professional wrestling pizzazz of being fixed.
1. Betting slips, fingerprints, handwriting, telephone records, sworn depositions— Come on! Let's have some real proof!

In October 1990, the *Late Show*'s Top Ten Lists had become so popular that a book of them was published by Pocket

Books. *USA Today* asked Letterman for his favorite ten Top Ten reasons.

Here is his list:

"Dave Letterman's Top Ten Top Ten Lists"

10. "Signs that Chef Boy-Ar-Dee Is Losing His Mind": Paranoid delusion that his wife is sleeping with Uncle Ben.
 9. "Pet Peeves of Indy 500 Pit Crews": It's hard to pick up chicks while reeking of methane.
 8. "Donahue Topics If Dogs Ran the Show": Dogs who use cat doors.
 7. "Things Overheard at the Moscow McDonald's": "In ten years, when you get a car, you'll appreciate the drive-through window."
 6. "Least Popular Ben & Jerry's Ice Cream Flavors": Stuff-Found-in-Ben-&-Jerry's-Pockets.
 5. "Terrifying Thoughts That Come to You as You're Falling Asleep": Could I get a rash on the *inside* of my skin?
 4. "Dan Quayle's National Guard Duties": Make sure Armory's vending machines never run out of pretzel sticks.
 3. "Things That Will Get You Kicked Out of Disney World": After biting into snack bar sandwich, saying, "I taste mouse."
 2. "Things Shirley MacLaine Was in Previous Lives": Confucius groupie.
 1. "John Gotti's Tax Tips": What H & R Block can't do, cement blocks can.

In July 1986, David Letterman appeared on the cover of *People* magazine. He had become a star by that time, having finished three years on NBC with *Late Night* at 12:30 and seemed ready to do at least three more.

His appearance as a cover celebrity elicited responses from readers, making up a new category that might be called "Top Four Letters from Readers":

4. From Dorothy Michalski, Turtle Creek, Pennsylvania. "What took you so long to put Letterman on the cover? David is the only guy I would ever seriously consider leaving my husband for. But the chances of that happening are not even worth figuring out, so go ahead and print my name."

3. From Diana Flory, Salinas, California: "Thinking it would be an endless task to pick your cover and the story behind it, from all the people that would be deserving such an honor. . . . David Letterman? Why not Regis Philbin? It would be a close second as to which one is more boring. Letterman can't sing or act. What made him think he could be a talk-show host? He need not worry about trying to ever compete with Johnny Carson's record. He's not even in the running, in my thinking. If NBC wants to keep him, stay with late, late night shows. After Johnny, I go to bed."

2. From Kellie Chamberline and Sarah Broderick, Bristol, Texas. "It's nice to know there are 3.7 million other people up till 1:30 in the morning watching a grown man jump onto a Velcro wall or doing other stupid human tricks."

1. From Robert del Valle, Troy, Michigan. "David Letterman is a living oxymoron (an insomniac's dream) and the best thing to happen to television since Ernie Kovacs. His early morning mirth is going to cost me my job one of these days—but I don't care!"

For some reason, David Letterman always loved to tease New York City about itself. Here are a number of gags that might be termed his "Top Four Jokes about New York":

4. "Interesting poll results were reported in today's *New York Post*: people on the street in midtown Manhattan were asked whether they approved of the U.S. invasion of Grenada. Fifty-three percent said yes; 39 percent said no; and 8 percent said 'Gimme a quarter?' "

3. "I couldn't be a bigger proponent of the subway system. So far I haven't been shot at, it takes eight minutes to get to work, it's relatively clean, and I must say that on each trip there's usually just one intimidating experience, so that's not too bad."

2. "The NBC studio is located in the center of Manhattan, midtown New York, New York—the town so nice they named it twice."

1. "It took me an hour and a half to get to work this morning, and I don't even live in the city!"

In 1988, the Writers Guild of America went on strike against the networks. It was particularly disconcerting to the television entertainment industry. David Letterman was forced to write even more jokes than he had previously. Herewith "Top Three Strike Jokes":

3. "It's the first time in memory that I've gotten so desperate to return to the talk-show business that I started to entertain people on street corners. Though they didn't seem to be truly *entertained*. Quietly, when they got home, perhaps they might admit that they were. Actually, just to get some TV time, I was shoplifting in 7-Elevens."

2. "The producers happen to be, in my opinion, money-grubbing scum. I want to make sure people understand I'm in favor of the Writers Guild [and its strike]."

1. "I am keeping busy during the Writers Guild strike with my gardening and phoning my favorite talk radio programs. Last month, I splurged and treated myself to much-needed liposuction surgery on my hips and thighs. I look and feel ten years younger."

In that same year David Letterman signed a deal with Walt Disney Studios to make a movie some time in the future. That led to a number of statements from Letterman about making this movie and about films in general. Here are "Top Four Comments by Dave about Movies":

4. "The movie deal, yeah. I'm going to get out there [in Hollywood] and make bad movies. That's what we need, is more of those six-dollar bombs. Actually, at the end of the contract period, if nothing has happened, I can give the money back to Disney. This is a 'movie deal' in the loosest interpretation of the phrase. At the meetings they don't say anything. There's some talk of me doing the kind of thing Buddy Ebsen used to do. At which period of his career? I don't really know. I go to those meetings, but I don't listen to anything."

3. "I'm really confident that one day I'll make a really bad movie. It will cost about $20 million, and many people who appear in the film with me will never work again."

2. "The deal, I think—I think—is still on. Money has changed hands. Yeah. And I think [Letterman laughs big] I think they would like it to change hands again."

1. "It just grinds me that I see the same stories—the same lines, the same chase scenes, the same 'we had a warm moment and now our lives are richer for it'—over, and over, and over again. Am I the only one who's noticed this, or are all movies the same because they're *supposed* to be the same?"

David Letterman traveled all over the country, and came to know the country well. Here are some "Top Nice Places to Visit, But—":

3. Once the *Late Show* spent two weeks in Burbank. The weather was gloomy even by San Fernando standards. Letterman tried to explain the reason to his staff. "It's a combination of two things. It's the shuttle launches, which are spewing unbelievable amounts of radiation into the Van Allen Belt. That, and the Soviets are doing some really curious, insidious meteorological testing, which will shorten our growing season, I would guess, down to like an afternoon. It's just a hunch, really."

2. Letterman was required to woo NBC affiliates in 1985 in order to strengthen the ratings of the *Late Show*.

"Wooing affiliates ranks somewhere near being dipped in suet and having owls turned loose on stage. Bringing the show to Los Angeles for two weeks on the other hand is a field trip, like when you were in high school and you went to see dentures being made."

1. "I try to get back to Indianapolis, my hometown, at least once a year. I enjoy the city. It's changed a lot, and it's only gotten nicer. The complaint that we always heard from outsiders was that it was a bit sleepy, which was fine with me. I don't mind sleepiness. Every time I go back, I'll always go to Steak 'n' Shake. I'll get two double cheeseburgers, some fries, and a vanilla shake— and be sick for days."

CHAPTER EIGHT
Late-Night Boomerangery

Not all David Letterman's highly touted pokes and jabs at celebrities and figures of renown proved to evoke boffo laughs from his viewers. At times his somewhat sophomoric jokes backfired badly. At other times he got into trouble not only with the public but with a higher authority.

Making fun of people in today's world is close to stepping over that very invisible and undetectable but important line of libel. And libel and defamation of character put heaps of money into the pockets of lawyers on both sides of the legal battlefield.

Inside the grown-up and seemingly mature David Letterman lurked that small cute little tyke from Broad Ripple whose day used to be made when he flashed blinding sunlight into unsuspecting drivers' eyes, who announced fake raffles at the supermarket, and who got people all panicky with phony fire drills. And occasionally that little boy surfaced and made life miserable for the matured human being in whom he continued to exist.

The first of the Big Insults aimed by David Letterman in his incarnation as *Late Night* caretaker at NBC was the host of NBC's popular *Today Show*. David Letterman happened to peer out the window of his office one morning and broke into a broad grin. Seven stories below, in Rockefeller Center, he saw Bryant Gumbel doing a live interview to be used on his show the next morning.

Letterman signaled his camera crew for action. And, as he picked up a bullhorn, he leaned out the window and yelled down with the amplifier on maximum LOUD:

"My name is Larry Grossman," the words boomed out raucously. "I am the president of NBC News." Up to that point, nothing unusual had happened. But Gumbel heard the noise and looked up with annoyance.

Then Letterman got into the core of the gag.

"And I'm not wearing any pants," he concluded.

Gumbel fumed. His interview was spoiled, and he had to start in again. Nevertheless, when the filmed piece was shown that night on *Late Night*, the audience howled with glee. So did the viewers. Gumbel glumly took the rap for Letterman's humor and seethed in private for some time after that.

"Bryant just hates me," Letterman admitted later. "He apparently is still angered by it. He really wanted to get into a fight or something."

Gumbel shrugged it off—to a degree. "If I'd had the opportunity to go after him physically, I would have. But I'm not that bad a grudge holder. I don't wander the halls looking for David Letterman."

No? Letterman complained later that he was never allowed to go on Gumbel's *Today Show* to plug his *Late Night*.

"I'm not surprised," Gumbel noted wryly. "We do do *some* screening around here."

Anyway, the axe was eventually buried.

But Gumbel wasn't the only one in for a taste of Letterman's acerbic wit. Nastassja Kinski, the actress, was scheduled to appear on the show one night. From the start, Letterman was nervous about interviewing her.

"I mean, what can you talk with her about? Her father is strange. We didn't want to get into her teenage relationship with Roman Polanski."

Fretting fitfully about what subject to pursue, Letterman looked up to observe her as she walked on. "Out she comes," he said later, "and it looks as if she has her hair wired around a nine iron."

Letterman was out of words for the moment. He kept looking at the electrified thing that was her coiffure. In the end he opted for humor.

"You've got to trust your instincts. My instincts said, 'This woman has a barn owl in her head; ask her about the barn owl.'"

Unfortunately, the hairdo was no joke. Kinski was hurt and then insulted. Suddenly the onus was on Letterman, who had treated her badly.

"I felt really uncomfortable," he admitted. Nevertheless, he went on, "You show up with your hair like a Douglas fir tree, you think, 'Well, here's a woman who's here for laughs.' It's never in my heart to think how I can mock guests on the show, but if there's something that lends itself to a silly remark, I'll probably try to make a joke out of it. You can't sit there with a bonsai tree on your head and not expect somebody to say something."

Letterman changed the subject and the talk continued in a different and more ordinary vein. Yet she was still flustered, and it showed.

"For about eight minutes, she was pretending that I was the one who was nuts," he said later.

And then, he went on, she happened to glance into the monitor and see herself as Letterman saw her. She grimaced and said, "Gee! I do look awful!"

That was vindication enough for Letterman, who had not truly intended to hurt her feelings.

Another target for Letterman's wit was George Will, the conservative writer. Will appeared to plug a book that he had just written. When Letterman asked him to describe the contents for the viewers briefly, Will went into a long and complicated outline of his material. The subject was the vicissitudes of the electoral college through the years.

Finally, Letterman noticed his studio audience dozing or beginning to stir restlessly, and he grinned and said:

"Do you seriously think anybody is going to buy this book?"

Not all of his viewers took kindly to that jibe at Will on national television.

Sometimes Letterman himself turned out to be the butt of the joke. No one succeeded in putting him on the spot the way Cher managed to do one night. She started out by confessing to him that she had been reluctant to appear on the show. Why? Because, she told him, she thought he was an "asshole."

Letterman, for once, was absolutely mute. He admitted later: "It *did* hurt my feelings. Cher was one of the few people I really wanted to have on the show. . . . I felt like a total fool, especially since I say all kinds of things to people. I was sitting there thinking, 'Okay, Mr. Big Shot, can you take it as well as you can dish it out?' " The obvious answer was that he could not.

Later on she sent him a note taking it all back and saying it was just a joke.

Shirley MacLaine managed to get in his hair, too. He could not get her to tell him ahead of time what she wanted to discuss on the show. She was "too big a star to do a preinterview" was the way he put it.

"We had no idea what she wanted to talk about. So the talent staff put together a list of four or five questions based on research material. Then she comes on the program and she brings with her an *attitude*, which she mentioned early on: 'I guess Cher was right.' "

Needless to say, the MacLaine interview, along with Cher's, did not go down in the annals of *Late Night* history as towering triumphs.

On his opening remarks early in September 1988 Letterman announced that Art Rooney, Sr., the owner of the Pittsburgh Steelers football team, had died. "Since it occurred during pro football's exhibition season, it led to some confusion as to whether the death actually counted." Letterman's intent was to poke fun at the nuances of pro football; instead, he seemed to be mocking the death of a beloved sports figure. The studio audience booed, and later Letterman told the people of Pittsburgh he was sorry. "It was not my intention to defame," he said.

At about the same time, he did a parody of a television commercial Martha Raye had done touting a denture powder. In the Letterman version, the commercial was about condoms. The implication was that Martha Raye was pushing condoms. She sued him and NBC for ten million dollars. She claimed that the use of her name had defamed her character. The case was settled out of court by NBC's legal staff.

A "Stupid Pet Trick" got the host of *Late Night* into hot water during the summer months. A dog named Randi, owned by Maryjane Kasian, wowed the audience one night by walking upright—on its two hind legs!—while balancing a glass of water on an upside-down Frisbee.

Later on Letterman appeared in July 1983 on *Evening Magazine*, a TV magazine show, where he talked about Randi's talents, and then said:

"The only thing that kind of detracts from that is [that] I know the woman has performed some sort of unethical and intricate spinal surgery on the dog, and that's illegal and she'll end up doing time. But as far as the trick goes, it's a ten."

When the Society for the Prevention of Cruelty to Animals showed up at Kasian's door, she launched a suit against Letterman, NBC, *Evening Magazine*, and others, claiming that Letterman's remarks had caused her "to suffer contempt and scorn and have impaired her standing in the eyes of a considerable and respectable class of the community."

The suit was finally settled by the NBC legals.

Another night the model Cheryl Tiegs was chatting with Letterman about a line of designer clothing sold in Sears. Letterman asked the obvious question: Did Tiegs herself wear the clothing?

Tiegs was miffed at the question, feeling that she was being put on the defensive for something she did not have to be defensive about.

Letterman pointed out: "If the person seems defenseless, you have no business getting in there and hurting their feelings. But if the person seems to be an incorrigible show-business buffoon, then I think they're a fair target."

Tiegs was not really any of the above, but Letterman did succeed in making his point with her.

Peter Ustinov visited the show one night, and launched into a rather long and tedious digression. Letterman listened for a while, and then broke in:

"Oh, you're imitating an English-speaking American, right?"

Not exactly the thing he should have said to Ustinov, who let him know it in no uncertain terms.

As to other Cher- and Shirley MacLaine-type put-downs, James Wolcott, in *Vanity Fair*, charged that David was acting "cranky" on his show. Letterman was far from tongue-tied at that attack. He responded with alacrity:

"To me, it was like criticizing Emmett Kelly because of his wardrobe." The crankiness, to David, was all part of his—well—charm.

Another writer, Peter W. Kaplan, had a long interview with Letterman for *Rolling Stone*, and related how the *Late Night* host had slammed the floor of his office with a baseball bat during the interview, raving about how low the standards of television were.

When he was asked why he had been batting the floor during the interview, Letterman thought a moment and then leaned back:

"I didn't like the way the guy was dressed."

Speaking of dressing, David Letterman claimed that he was always being put down sartorially by the people close to him. He cited Merrill Markoe's mother as one of them. She did not like the way this grown man who lived with her daughter always came to the house in jeans and a T-shirt.

"Merrill's mother," Letterman said, "says she watches [the show] just to see me in a suit."

A critic named Monica Collins joined Wolcott in describing Letterman as "cranky" and, at the same time, "bored."

Letterman's response: "So now I'm supposed to be cheerful all the time? As a matter of fact, that's one of the things I really do enjoy, from five-thirty to six-thirty each day. When it goes well, there's no greater fun to be had. And even if I appear cranky or pessimistic or grouchy on the show, I always thought that was kind of a source of fun. Here's a guy who is not omni-cheerful. Why pretend you're feeling good when you've got a cold?"

As an afterthought, Letterman observed, "I'd like to slap that Monica Collins."

To which Collins responded, "I'd like to slap that David Letterman. I'd like to kick him. Especially when he's down."

Once Steve Martin was on the show, and he and Letterman were gabbing about this and that in an indeterminate way. Martin suddenly thought of something that had been bothering him.

"Can I ask you a question?"

Letterman indicated that he could.

"When you drive to work, does NBC pay or do you have to drive yourself?"

Letterman pondered that a moment. "It's something that perhaps could be negotiated."

"The reason I'm asking is, I happen to be friendly with NBC."

Letterman smiled. "You'd be the only one."

The wide-ranging nature of the putdowns on the show constantly left him open to all kinds of counterattacks by public relations experts on the lookout for just such insults— especially if they happened to be in error.

One such backfire occurred in September 1993, when Letterman claimed inaccurately that American bottles of Heineken beer were being recalled for containing particles of glass. His joke focused on the fact that the faulty bottles were being relabeled "chunky style." It was an okay joke. But it just so happened that the premise was untrue.

In the end, Letterman succeeded in turning the jest back on himself. He had just moved from 12:30 A.M. to 11:30 P.M. "Mr. Big Shot wanted to be on at 11:30," he said deprecatingly. "At 12:30, we could say all kind of stuff that wasn't true."

David Letterman went through a period when he was arrested for speeding several times by state troopers in New York and Connecticut, where he had his home. Every arrest was accompanied by nationwide coverage in the press. If one had not heard of what David Letterman was, it would be obvious that he was a notorious speeder.

That led Jeff Colburn, a reporter on the *San Francisco Chronicle* to write in his predictions for 1989: "David Letterman and Zsa Zsa Gabor will strike up a curious but mutually satisfying relationship after meeting in traffic school."

Even on his own show Letterman could find himself topped after an exchange of one kind or another. Michael Jordan, then the Chicago Bull's star basketball player, was on the show one night when Letterman asked the by-now familiar question:

"Are you the tallest in your family?"

"Yes. I'm six six, and everybody else in the family is about five eight or five nine." Pause. "But the milkman is about six seven."

One afternoon Phil Donahue invited him on his show, and Letterman obliged. There he was subjected to a number of old tapes of shows he had done in Indiana, things he had done on the morning show, acquaintances from his past in Indianapolis, and all sorts of memorabilia.

"Boy, was it strange!" he said after it was all over. "Phil used to get such great audiences in Chicago, but what he's getting here [now] are flood victims. I knew it would be a long hour, and boy, was it ever!" (It will be remembered that at one point Letterman injected the pointed question that implied terminal boredom on the show: "Is this one of those special ninety-minute shows, Phil?") "It was so bizarre, my heart sank. I just wanted to go home."

And he did go home—eventually.

Even at home he was subject to personal attack. "We're the two worst social people ever," Merrill Markoe said time and again. "This is *not* life in the fast lane."

As if to prove that point in a much more pungent manner, an organization called International Dull Folks Unlimited selected David Letterman for its Number One Bore Award in the year 1987—Number One in its list of Ten Dullest Americans. In its citation, the reason given for the award was as follows:

"What more can be said of a TV host who can't get on the air until after midnight and whose shtick is a Stupid Pet Trick?"

The counterattacks and the verbal abuse to which David Letterman was being subjected actually ran off him like water off a duck's back—once he had made a point of showing publicly how upset he pretended to be. He later laid it all to part of the so-called learning process. And he mentioned how it affected his actions on his own *Late Night* show.

"I think what we've learned is that for us, the simpler ideas work better than the overblown ideas. For example, we called my mother to place a Super Bowl bet with her. To me, that idea has more appeal now than it probably would have had the first year [of the show]. To me, it just seems more pure, more genuine. Let's do smaller ideas and get bigger results, as opposed to a big idea that may not work. There's not much on TV that's going to surprise people."

One of his favorite pastimes was to compare the ongoing show with its earliest days.

"I think what has come over the years is a more consistent spirit. We have more confidence now in what we do. Whereas before it was like rolling a hand grenade into a hen house— you just waited to see where the feathers would land." Pause. "You know, that's not a bad idea, rolling a hand grenade into . . . Nah!"

CHAPTER NINE
The Letterman Persona

David Letterman was once talking about what he considered to be one of his most valuable assets or talents as a person: resourcefulness.

"I'm very resourceful," he observed. "I'd be good in prison. I'd be good in a shipwreck. I'd make a great hostage. Oh, I have talents aplenty. Unfortunately, precious few of them have any redeeming social value."

He was speaking, of course, with tongue firmly planted in cheek. The question naturally does arise, what then are his redeeming features? Does he have any? What kind of person is he really? What is the true Letterman persona?

Of all his talents, resourcefulness may be very high on the list. But it is not his most redeeming feature. His ability to put himself down, in other words, his talent for self-mockery, strikes one as his most predominant and important character trait. From it all else flows.

Letterman has always been a real fan of auto racing, largely stemming from the fact that his birthplace is also the birthplace of the Indy 500. He used to travel all over the country to catch what auto races he could.

Once, in Phoenix, the wife of a good friend introduced him to Paul Newman, according to a *Playboy* interview. Newman himself was a fan of auto racing, and a driver as well. He owned a stable of racing cars.

"He was cordial and genuine and gracious and it was great fun," Letterman said.

The two men talked about racing for half an hour, and after that Letterman would bump into him at almost every racing event he would go to. Since Letterman had met him formally, that meant that he could say hello to him wherever he saw him.

Well, he tried it.

Unfortunately, without the help of someone who was a friend to each of them, Letterman was unable to make contact with Newman. What he called Newman's "radar deflection screen" was always in the UP position. Newman was as shy a man as Letterman himself, although Letterman never seemed to consider that a possibility.

Instead, he kept trying to make contact with him.

The more he tried, the more obvious it became that Newman was *not* going to relate to Letterman in public, or even to admit that he shared the same planet with him.

There was a race out at the Meadowlands in New Jersey in the metropolitan area. Letterman was seated at a table under a big tent that was serving as the hospitality suite. Up roared Paul Newman on a motor scooter, parking it with a flourish outside. Joanne Woodward, Newman's famous wife, appeared and mounted the scooter behind her husband.

The Newmans were so close to Letterman he could have touched them.

"Paul!" yelled Letterman. "It's me, Dave! Dave Letterman!"

The Newmans drove off without a flicker of recognition from Paul. "I could have been in China," Letterman recalled ruefully.

Later on, Dave would be with friends at one race or another when Paul Newman would suddenly surface. Once Letterman nudged a friend as they walked down a pit lane, and said, "Hey, watch this!"

Paul Newman was coming over. "Paul! Paul!" Letterman waved his arms. "Paul!"

No sign of recognition. "Paul! Paul!" Letterman waved his arms. "Paul!"

No sign of anything at all. The radar deflection screen was definitely up.

One year, Letterman was climbing up into the timing and scoring tower at the Indianapolis 500, and there, approaching him in full view, was Paul Newman, coming down. At last!

They almost touched elbows. But nothing. Not a flicker in those blue, blue eyes. "It was like he'd been struck mute and deaf. I was so tickled by this dynamic," Letterman noted.

Translation: tickled, no doubt. But pleased?

The last time he saw Paul Newman was 1992 at a race in Ohio. Letterman and his girlfriend were in an elevator, crowded as hell. Paul Newman was right next to them. There wasn't room enough for anybody to move.

"Paul!" Letterman called. "Paul. It's me. Dave. Paul?"

As the elevator came to a stop, everybody walked off in their own separate directions. Likewise Paul Newman.

Newman's partner in the auto-racing gig was a man named Carl Hass. He was a cigar smoker, and that made him mates with Letterman. Every so often Letterman would mail Hass a box of good cigars.

The last time Letterman saw Hass, he put a proposition to him.

"I don't care how long it takes, but before I die, could you have Paul Newman, just once, once more, say hi to me?"

Of course, Hass nodded his head.

And sure enough, two days later, the telephone rang in Letterman's office. It was Paul Newman.

NEWMAN: I didn't know you liked auto racing.

LETTERMAN: Paul, you and I met six years ago in Phoenix. Ever since then, I've been screaming at you whenever I see you.

NEWMAN: Is that so?

LETTERMAN: So I just wondered—

NEWMAN: Wondered what?

LETTERMAN (sighing): Never mind.

This story does have a happy ending, which will be revealed in due time. But for the nonce, it is interesting to analyze this incident from the life of David Letterman. It is, of course, the perfect and classic example of the little man being brushed aside by the big man. Essentially, it is the essence of comedy, the essence that especially the great Charlie Chaplin managed to capture time and time again.

The object of self-mockery is to elicit sympathy from the person who hears it or observes it. Whenever the comic is put down, laughter ensues, usually at the comic's expense. Nevertheless, every time the laugher laughs, he pays something in sympathy for the comic.

When the little impish boy inside David Letterman's frame pulls a fast one, Letterman is protected by the fact that David Letterman has honed his persona to perfection over the years. He is the be-all and the end-all of the self-mocking man.

When he shoots an arrow into the balloon of self-esteem that is the typical blowhard bigshot, he fires it from down below—not from up above. If the arrow came from above, the balloon burst would not be half so funny: it would elicit a grim nod of self-righteousness. Coming from below, it encourages the observer to clap his hands and exclaim: "Right on!" Also to laugh. Unrestrainedly. The worm has turned. Long live the worm.

Self-mockery is the key element of Letterman's complicated personality. It is the one that makes him successful, memorable, and comic.

He is, however, a complicated fellow. For that reason he has been called many different things, and in a serious, analytical way. He has been called psychotic, gloomy, self-effacing, derogatory, juvenile, whimsical, goofy, intellectual, impulsive, off-the-wall, pontifical, deadpan, pessimistic, cynical, neurotic, steady, and oddball; he has been characterized as a smart-ass, a show-off, a comedy snob, a natural wit, a cult favorite, a sport, a humorist, and a hopeless nerd.

He was once asked if he was a hard man to work for. "Oh, yeah. I'm a terror. I have—what do you call them?—psychotic mood swings. Psychotic temper tantrums. I'm nefariously moody. I'm a tyrant. I'm incorrigible."

"That may be true, yet your staff members seem rather happy."

"Those are all actors brought in for your benefit."

Letterman always seemed to sink into deep pits of gloom when things were going good. Why? "It's because I'm nuts. I need professional help. And I need it *now*."

To a woman who claimed to be the smartest person in the world: "If you're so smart," Letterman riposted, "how come you aren't doing something *important* right now?"

Publicity once described a trick Letterman was going to do for a TV special as a "heart-stopping thrill." The trick involved being dressed in Velcro and then catapulted onto a thirty-foot wall of the stuff to hang there like a fly.

"It's far from heart-stopping, unless you've got one of those faulty Jarvik deals," Letterman noted.

After that, the publicity said, on would come the Rockettes from the Radio City Music Hall.

"When they come out, these thirty-six very leggy women all lined up in their little goose outfits or whatever they are, and they start the kick line, as corny as it sounds, it's like watching fireworks. You just go, oh wow! And then the show goes down-hill from there."

About his work: "Much of the stuff I do is adolescent stuff—like junior high school kids on a rainy day who send pizzas to the substitute teacher."

About the universe around us: "There are other things going on in the universe besides a nightly talk show. And there may even be other realities beyond this universe. For all we know, our entire universe may exist in a styrofoam beer cooler in somebody's garage."

Did he ever send important sociopolitical messages out with his humor? "I guess I don't have the sensitivity or the intellec-tual capacity to be using humor as a conduit for some loftier message. I'm right there in dead-center silliness, goofiness, you know, kind of pointless comedy; and for me, that's a pretty tall load."

Most of Letterman's writers on *Late Night* were Harvard graduates. "I love pushing these Ivy league boys around. I went to a state school and these guys are working for me. That's America, isn't it?"

He has been said to be malicious on the air. "It's a boorish thing we're doing. . . . There are people who perceive what I do as cruel, but I'm not malicious. I don't want to get a laugh at the expense of others. Then again, if I see an opening, I go for it.

"My problem is if I see a place to say something funny I'll say something funny. If the guest is Hugh Hefner, people assume he can take care of himself. If it's a woman who's been an usher at a theater for thirty years, then maybe it's perceived as being cruel. I always try to be careful when we have civilians on, but I admit I do shoot first and ask questions later."

He once explained how he had become a professional comic. "Oddly enough, I was drafted. I was forced to go to California and become a comedian. I wrote my congressman, but nothing would help."

He had nothing against fat people, he explained at one time. "I must say, I watched that Connie Chung documentary about fat people, and I was always under the impression that fat people were fat because they would sit down in front of the TV with a bag of Kraft caramels and eat them just until they were gone. And as it turns out—this is the lesson I learned from the lovely Connie—that is not the case. And so as a result of that I have tried to enlighten myself regarding fat people. But even prior to that I never *disliked* fat people. So I'm working on this. I'm trying to grow here."

Some questioned as to whether or not he considered his boredom threshold unusually low. "No, I don't think so. I am fascinated by all manner of minutiae and trivia. [If I *appear* bored,] I've made a terrible mistake. It means I've lost control of myself. . . . But I tell you, I see this in my mother. She is the least demonstrative person I've ever been around. . . . Her countenance will reveal no interest, no stimuli, no response, nothing. Then you ask her about it and she gets angry because, of course, she is paying rapt attention and is following the conversation."

He always worries when things are going well. "I suffer from anhedonia. . . . I think the exercise is the struggle. If life isn't hard, you're doing something wrong. Don't you think? And I'll sleep when I'm dead."

To him, show business is based on the genetic crapshoot that makes some people beautiful and the bulk of us ugly. "When I think about television and show business, it grinds my stomach. I want to say to people, 'Don't you understand this is just bullshit, driven by egos, and that's all it is?' I mean, nothing makes me madder than to be sitting there, watching somebody who's just the winner of the genetic crapshoot, and there they are, big stuff and on the air, a *star*."

He makes mistakes, too. "You say something, and the second it leaves your mouth you think, 'Oohhh, if I had just given it a second more consideration, I wouldn't be suffering this embarrassment now.' I have a very low threshold of self-embarrassment. I do things I'm very upset by, and not very many things I'm pleased by. But I just think that's part of the general neurosis that motivates people to go into show business. I've had this job longer than any other job I've ever had. When you do that, you become more focused and more introverted than maybe is a good idea. So I think that's caused me to change a bit."

It's an attitude problem, maybe. "It's never been my intention to cause ill will among the fraternity and sorority of celebrities. I think some people may feel that they're not being treated with enough respect or that their work is diminished through some flip attitude on my part. But I'm a wise-ass and a smart-ass, and I always have been."

As to what kind of person he is, "I'm the kind of guy that on a hot day, if a neighbor comes over and needs help installing a through-the-window air-conditioner . . . I'll be there."

What makes him *really* laugh? "A couple of months ago, for no reason, we made waffles, as an adjunct activity to the show. I liked having a show and then, every few minutes, seeing if the waffles were done. I don't know why exactly."

Letterman admits to being a comedy snob. "I could count [the few truly funny guys] on one hand. I just wonder if, like expansion in major-league baseball, it doesn't tend to water down the product."

Having a conversation with David Letterman can be an adventure in arriving back at the starting gate without even running the race.

COSMO: You said, "I feel like a million bucks," in your opening monologue. How does a million bucks feel?

LETTERMAN: Beats me. I'm just tickled by the phrase.

COSMO: You're saying you've yet to feel like a million bucks during any of this?

LETTERMAN: Oh, no, I'm embarrassed by all the attenton.

COSMO: So what kind of dollar value would you place on how you feel?

LETTERMAN: I feel like a million bucks.

About being a cult favorite: "They used to call us a cult favorite. I always thought that meant: 'Nobody's watching.' "

About performing as a talk-show host: "Anyone who has done standup can do this. It's like being able to lay down a bunt."

Cybill Shepherd sent her dress to the studio a week ahead of her visit to the *Late Night* show. Letterman and NBC used the incident to promote her appearance ahead of time. Not to be outdone, Shepherd arrived wrapped in a large towel, pretending that she had no dress on at all.

"It seemed appropriate," she said. "Most talk-show hosts only want to score points at the guest's expense, but David's humor comes from the situation."

In a piece he wrote for the *New York Times* in February 1993, Frank Rich summed up a number of the important elements of David Letterman's persona, and thus of his humorous zeitgeist. "He ostentatiously mispronounces his guests' names, leaves jokes unfinished, fumbles the file cards containing his gags, garbles his guests' movie titles."

All these details, of course, were standard putdowns. Not to know a celebrity's name put one up on the celebrity, proving that the celeb was not *that* celeb-rated. Even leaving jokes unfinished was a tribute to the viewer's supersophistication—"doesn't even need the punchline to get the joke." Garbling movie titles was a putdown game in itself, such as "that unforgettable movie classic *Gone with the Wine.*"

Rich pointed out that "weeks after the 1992 election he persisted in calling the new First Lady 'Valerie.'" And he mentioned Letterman's mocking of Shirley MacLaine's spiritual beliefs and termed most of his comedy recycled practical jokes from adolescence.

"Letterman benefits . . . from his WASP cool, which still impresses a multicultural public as long as it is Midwestern Carson WASP-iness rather than the discredited patrician brand of George Bush."

"Cool" accordingly meant Letterman would get dates in high school by telling the girls he would rather stay home. He never ran for office because he knew conspicuous good citizenship was a joke, so said Rich. "He would say he inhaled during the sixties whether he did or not," Rich concluded.

An epitaph once suggested by David Letterman for his tombstone read as follows:

DAVID LETTERMAN. HE WASN'T FUNNY, BUT HE WASN'T AN ASSHOLE.

CHAPTER TEN
The Wife Action

One morning recently David Letterman was being interviewed on *CBS This Morning* by Paula Zahn and the subject
of marriage came up. The question that followed most naturally was a perennial one: with whom was Letterman going
out—or, to put it more bluntly in 1990's terms—with whom
was he living?

Letterman clammed up. He did not want it known whom
he was "dating" because he inadvertently had once told a
magazine article writer the name of his current significant
other—with disastrous results.

"Are you seeing someone?" the interviewer had asked.

"Oh, yes, yes," Letterman told him.

"Who?"

Letterman revealed "who" and then added where she had
come from and where her family still lived.

"And then, you know, people started following her around,
people started calling her, people started bothering her
parents."

Letterman was nonplussed.

He thought, "That seems like a mistake. These people are
just going about their lives, and there are folks sitting in rental
cars out in front of their house."

Letterman: "It was a learning experience for me. No more of that."

And so Zahn sighed and said: "So, let's not talk about the wife action then."

That intrigued Letterman. His face lighted up. " 'The wife action?' Is *that* how you refer to it?"

Zahn suggested another subject to talk about, but Letterman wouldn't let go of a good phrase.

"No. Let's talk about 'the wife action.' "

But they did not. They talked about the subject of having children instead.

Nevertheless, the women in the life of David Letterman have always fascinated fans, nonfans, and almost everybody else. They fall into three categories: his one and only wife; his live-ins; and the unexpected guest at his home in New Canaan.

In addition, of course, there are his mother and his two sisters. In spite of the fact that most people rarely associate Letterman with a family, he has always remained very close to both sisters. They are Janice, now a married mother of two living in Indiana, and Gretchen, also married and the mother of one. Gretchen is an editorial writer for Florida's *St. Petersburg Times.*

He remains close to his mother, too—very close. He usually wanders into the Midwest at least two or three times a year, once especially during the time of the Indy 500 in Indianapolis. When he is in Indiana, he always visits his mother.

Last year, he said, he got to her place about 8:30 P.M.

"David," his mother asked him, "would you like some strawberry pie?"

Letterman walked into the kitchen and spotted a fresh-baked strawberry pie on the table.

"When did you make this?" he asked his mother.

"I started right after I got off the phone with you."

Letterman: "It was just the cutest. I was so touched. Isn't that motherhood? She gets off the phone, drops what she's doing, and *bakes a pie.*"

Very little has been written about David Letterman's only wife, Michelle, whom he married during his college days at

Ball State. She appears early in the story of his life, and although he was married to her for almost ten years, she does fade out of the limelight at about the time Letterman was beginning to make an impact on show business.

Her name, as has been related, is Michelle Cook. In the Letterman saga, her presence tends to be a sometime thing. He never says anything bad about her or about marriage. Nevertheless, his concept of marriage tends not to be entirely positive.

"Oh, I'll get married again," he told an interviewer recently. "You see, the thing is, I was married for ten years. So I know the good parts of it and I know the bad parts. If it were up to me, I'd have children out of wedlock. But I know that's not the best way to approach it."

"With whom?"

"Well, let's see who's waiting downstairs." The Letterman grin. Followed by the Letterman glower. "Now, don't print that, goddamn it!"

At the time Michelle became part of his past, Letterman had just met Merrill Markoe. The two of them were performers at the Comedy Store.

She, too, was interested in writing as well as performing comedy.

But the two were hardly alike. They were opposites in many ways.

"She is verbal and uncompromising about what is worth pursuing [in life]. She is intelligent. Nothing like I am."

"We're both intense, neurotic people who worry about everything and expect the worst," Merrill added. "Dave is the most competitive person I have ever spent a lot of time with. It really matters to him to win *everything* he goes into."

A graduate of the University of California at Berkeley, Merrill came away with a major in fine arts, started to teach school in Los Angeles, and then quit.

Once she met Letterman they both knew that they made a good professional team. Merrill worked as a writer for the Mary Tyler Moore 1977 variety show. When Letterman's short-lived morning talk show began, she became its head writer. Then for the first years of *Late Night* she was head writer there, too.

"I seemed a logical choice. I had been trained to reflect his comedy."

After four or five years she gave up the writing job in favor of working as Letterman's associate producer. What she specialized in were film clips done on location. The originator of Letterman's famed "Stupid Pet Tricks," she handled every one of them.

But tension began building between the two of them soon enough. What Merrill wanted to do—and what David Letterman to his credit never tried to stop her from doing—was write something to come out of a mouth other than Letterman's.

Letterman understood. He had always respected her intelligence and her energy.

"She's the funniest person I've ever met," he said. "And she's so smart it's scary. I mean, she'll walk into a room and you can *feel* a hum coming out of her brain."

At one time he had said, "If either Merrill or I get married, it will probably be to each other."

Was the "probably" Letterman's prophetic vision of the future?

"We were working on that show and then went home, and instead of having a life, we were still working on the show. . . . Every day at work was a fistfight. Every night at home was a fistfight. Figuratively speaking."

And it had to come to an end. "She wanted to put some of the energy that she was putting into me and my life and my show and my career—she wanted to do the same for herself."

Finally, she told him, "I just can't."

She had never wanted to come to New York anyway. She had done it for Letterman. Now when things began to fall apart, she told him frankly: "I have to go back to California."

As Merrill put it: "You don't want your boyfriend making all the decisions about your work. I was in daily battle with him."

And so the ideal live-in couple of the entertainment business broke up in the way many such breakups occur. It was a slow ending to a long affair, Letterman pointed out. He continued to see Merrill even after she had moved to California. But by then it was all over. Both of them knew it.

When last questioned, she said that she "wouldn't even talk to people about working on another late-night show. I have no interest in helping any other white man in a suit do an inventive show. Let them all find their own damn inventive shows."

As for her, she had settled down to writing books. Period.

David commented in typical Letterman style about that statement: "You'll never get me to say anything bad about Merrill. She's the smartest, funniest woman I've ever been around. I have nothing but good things to say about [her], and she can say anything she wants about me and it won't trouble me."

So be it.

David Letterman's marriage to Michelle Cook was a personal relationship. His relationship with Merrill Markoe was a professional and personal one. What relationship followed that one was and is his business. *Time* magazine had it recently that the woman in question currently, after Merrill, was named "Regina Lasko," but Letterman mentioned that fact only once in public—and regretted even that mention of it soon enough.

Throughout his years with Merrill Markoe, Letterman was chary of experimenting a second time with the marriage situation—"the wife action." Which always put him in an ambivalent position. He was suspicious of marriage because of what it had done to him and to Michelle. But at the same time, he had always wanted to have a family.

"I would love to have kids," he said. "I would absolutely love to have kids, and I will. I will get to it. . . . A couple of years ago my friends all started having babies, and I was charmed by this. I hadn't been around an infant in years and years and years. And, man!—was that a pleasant experience. Just the way they feel, just the weight of them, the way they kind of move, and the hair."

He frowned. "You just put your face right up on the baby's head, and there's nothing like that. Have you ever felt anything like that? . . . This is something I have to do."

But he had a sudden thought. "God knows, I'm only marginally able to take care of *myself*. What if I suddenly got the kid's head caught in a revolving door?"

Sigh. "It's sad that at [my] age I can still be that silly about an important subject."

But the fact remained that David Letterman was shy of being once again burned in a way that had left such a scar on his psyche. "My life is so different now from what it was then that it does seem strange that there was this other person with whom I was very close for all that time [and] who now plays no part in my life."

The fact of the matter is that women have always, and still do, make him nervous in certain circumstances. Some women, that is. "Sure. But for a variety of reasons. If it's somebody I don't know, if that person herself is nervous, if I am ill-prepared to conduct any kind of intelligent exchange, yeah."

As for sexual entanglements, Letterman never considered it much of a problem, except at the beginning. The American lifestyle had changed enough in the years he was growing up so that he did not feel embarrassed anymore. "In the beginning, I was uncomfortable about it, and I don't know why, except that I've always been kind of shy, and I felt that people probably didn't want to see me on the air, period, let alone see me on the air talking about my private life.

"I've found that the one area I'm always uncomfortable talking about is—uh—female companions. Because I've never been able to reference that area without pissing someone off. It never comes easy. You can just sort of hear the clock ticking before it comes up as a topic."

He went into his imitation of a savvy and hip interviewer about to ask him to reveal all the secrets of his sex life.

"Soooo. I understand that. . . ."

And then, his bumbling answer: "Well, no, it wasn't like *that*, I didn't mean that, you see it—"

He shrugged. "So I thought for my own preservation I'd just skip it."

It was an interviewer for an article in *Playboy* who put him through the hoops. For starters, the writer began:

"Do you want to talk about your sexual history?"

"Well, no, I don't. What is *wrong* with you?"

"We have to get some sex into this. Do you want to talk about the first time?"

"No, no, I don't."

"The second time? No one ever talks about the second time."

"The second time hasn't happened yet!"

That riposte effectively blocked the interviewer, who glided on to another subject. And yet in the back of his mind, the interviewer knew he had to supply some of the commodity the magazine for which he was doing the story was famous for.

He had suggested to Letterman that being on television, appearing before millions of people, was life times ten, magnified and amplified.

Letterman agreed. "It's certainly the most exciting hour of the day, and it's the only hour of the day I really care about. And if it goes well, you can't wait to do it again, because it dumps so much adrenaline into your system. If it's going well, it just lifts you. If it's not going well, it sinks you. It's exhilarating. It's my favorite hour of the day."

"Better than sex?" asked the interviewer slyly, thinking about his check for services rendered.

"Well, speak for yourself," Letterman replied stiffly. "Is it better than sex? I'd say it's certainly comparable. I think if it goes well, the afterglow sustains you *more* than sex."

And so in the Letterman philosophy of life, there *were* things in life better than sex!

An interview with Ann Landers in *USA Today* said that most women preferred hugging to actual sexual intercourse. This interview was reprinted everywhere, and became a cause célèbre in the press and on television.

The reason for the interest was the obvious disagreement by millions of American women. They said that women who wanted hugging rather than real sex were obviously out of touch with life. That is, they were not only wrong, they had simply dropped out of the twentieth century altogether.

With the battleground strewn already with dead bodies of

psychologists, philosophers, and columnists of all kinds and stripes, David Letterman felt it was time for him to make his preferences known.

Instead, he came up with this opener one night.

"You know, for the longest time there I thought hugging *was* intercourse. So it was a revelation to me to find out it was two different things. What I found was [that] it wasn't as hard on your clothing, so I continued to do it."

As for *talking* about sex, that was an even harder game. He admitted that Dr. Ruth Westheimer did embarrass him— "with all her talk of clitorises and penises."

That brought on a rejoinder from Dr. Ruth as follows:

"[David] stumbles every time he has to say the word *orgasm*. But he's getting better."

She did not specify what he was getting better at doing, leaving the statement open-ended for any interpretation desired.

Nevertheless, David Letterman was never able to rid himself completely of his apparently ingrown midwestern inability to chat superficially and extendedly about sex in a physical sense—naming the organs, and so forth.

One of his best friends in the comedy business, Jeff Altman, made a guest appearance on *Late Night* some years ago. During the interview he made a lewd crack, as he recalled it, about sex that included the word "genitals."

Letterman did not laugh.

Altman called David on his silence later in the evening when the two were eating dinner together.

"You could have helped me out a little there," Altman said.

Letterman looked directly at Altman. "Maybe you shouldn't have said that on TV."

David Letterman himself has always been an object of interest to women—an object of sexual interest, for that matter. In fact, many women believe him to be just about every woman's dream. When that fact was put to him, Letterman smiled and said:

"Yeah. You'd think so, wouldn't you?" There was a pause. "But I'm no day at the beach, let's just say that."

CHAPTER ELEVEN
Celebrities Anonymous

"My name is Dave. I am a celebrity."

No such announcement ever took place at a meeting of Celebrities Anonymous, or ever will, given the fact that such an organization does not exist, or ever will. But there is a good deal of truth in the concept—held by most Americans—that being a celebrity is something akin to being a gambler, a liar, and a cheat, or an alcoholic unable to avoid the highs and lows of ongoing substance abuse.

The very act of being a celebrity puts one at a tremendous advantage—and at the same time an inordinate disadvantage—in his or her relationship with the rest of the world. Many celebrities opt to associate only with other celebrities, at least to the extent that such a prospect is attainable. Others opt to associate literally with no one other than those people who are in their specific area of ability or expertise.

Thus Jay Leno associates with scores of stand-up comics—or, at least, he used to before becoming the star of the *Tonight Show*. Film actors and actresses tend to socialize and party with other film actors and actresses. So do TV performers. Sports figures blessed with great ability and enormous emolument tend to flock together with others exactly like them.

There are some, mostly in a minority, who choose to associate with no one at all. These are the recluses, the celebrities whom everyone talks about but no one sees. These are the ones who keep to themselves.

From the beginning David Letterman tended to play it close to the vest, always making it a point not to run with the "big" people in his days in Indianapolis. As has been noted, he did not date the prettier girls in his high school class, but instead joined other misfits and threw eggs at their houses.

And with success he did not change one iota. In fact, his chief asset as a talk-show host on *Late Night with David Letterman* was to puncture the pretenses of other celebrities and the rich and famous. Because of that fact, he did not find it easy to associate in a buddy-buddy fashion with most of them at all.

"There aren't many people in show business I really admire," he said once, although he immediately backtracked and admitted that there were exceptions. The most notable in this category was Johnny Carson.

And yet he always managed to keep his distance from him, too. "Johnny Carson has always been very nice to me, and obviously very helpful, but he just scares me silly. I can't relax with him because he's been such a presence in my life from the time I was in high school. I feel like I'm going to go to his house and I'm going to turn around and knock a vase over. And then of course Ed [McMahon] will have to come in and clean it up. Now Ed, you can relax around. Ed's like watching a guy take a nap."

He once admitted to Peter Lassally that he was frightened out of his wits around Carson. Lassally, an executive producer on the Carson show and also a producer on the Letterman show, which Carson coproduced, acted in an informal capacity as friend and career adviser for Letterman.

Dave commiserated, "I'm always afraid he'll say something to me like, 'Let's play tennis this weekend.' I'm terrified of actually spending time with him."

Lassally was less than understanding about this hangup. "Oh, grow up, asshole!" he told Letterman.

But Dave stuck to his guns. "The thing about appearing on

the *Tonight Show* is that any time could be your last time out. They're not particularly sympathetic to a weak appearance."

However, he eventually did go to Carson's house for a tennis game. "I was defeated, six to one," Letterman said. "Under the circumstances, I did give it my all. I just couldn't get over the fact that you look across the net and there's Johnny Carson! I just never got beyond that."

Afterward, when they went into Carson's tennis house— "What I really mean is 'Olympic venue' "—Letterman kept thinking he would have to get out of there before he punched a hole in one of Carson's drums sheerly by accident. "I just couldn't get out of there quick enough. He was very nice, but I was just out of control."

Eventually, both David Letterman and Johnny Carson were on the cover of *Rolling Stone* magazine together. And it was then that Letterman had his final say on Johnny Carson.

"I'm much taller than Carson," he said pointedly. "They had him on a box, goddamn it! . . . The truth comes out. He was on a box!"

Although what Letterman thought, and thinks, about Sandra Bernhard never did come out, her appearance on his *Late Night* show during its early months in 1982 was a breakthrough of one kind or another. The fact that she was teamed with Madonna made it even more of a viewer enhancement.

Peter W. Kaplan called it "the Sandra Bernhard-Madonna episode, a fiery little landmark on late-night television." He also wrote that "the Madonna scenario was equal to the best car-crash encounters that Jack Paar [ever] managed to create."

Bernhard came on the show dressed in dungaree shorts and a T-shirt. When Letterman got up to greet her, she locked herself to him and gave him a long, hard, grinding French kiss that lasted for at least five full seconds. Letterman was struggling to maintain some kind of decor at this point, but he seemed visibly shaken.

His guest plowed right on ahead, attacking a number of her critics in a nonstop diatribe. She even played on the air the tape of a telephone message one of them had delivered.

"The show was," Kaplan said, "within milliseconds, as dangerous as great television comedy should be."

Then Bernhard called on her friend Madonna, who came out in a déjà vu sequence, dressed identically in dungaree shorts and a T-shirt. The viewer could not help but feel locked into some kind of zany time warp.

The two women began kidding each other and kidding Letterman, who at this point was beginning to realize what he had here, and he began rolling with their punches, starting to enjoy himself. Unconsciously, he reached for one of the huge cigars he always has around, and then had the camera pull up on himself to regain control of the show.

But Letterman understood that a historic connection of sorts had been made—and a good one. "We haven't had her in a while," he noted recently, "because she and I sort of wore each other down. We had maybe done it too many times. She's very nice. The only thing we've ever really wanted from anybody is that they just sit down, start talking, and take over, for God's sake.

"And Sandra is good in that sense. I mean, we're continually surprised by people in show business who come out and don't seem to have any idea that the proceeding is being televised. Although I guess you could make a case for that."

Sometimes the celebrities on the Letterman show were somewhat puzzled over occurrences that took place. Teri Garr told about some of her experiences. "It's weird," she said. "I'll be on the show, and he'll push a note right under my face. And it'll say, 'I HATE MYSELF.' So I'll say, 'No, no, Dave, you're wonderful.' And he'll take it back and underline 'I HATE MYSELF' twice and push it back. What's that about?"

Letterman never did explain what he was trying to get at. But he did remark generally about the many changes in comedy since the days he started out in Indianapolis.

"I think I'm getting to be like my parents," he said. "It seems like attitude and style are taking the place of things that are actually funny. Steve Martin is brilliant. But it's like an entire generation saw his Wild and Crazy Guy [act] and thought, 'I get it! All I have to do to be funny is put an arrow through my head!'

"And of course they had it all wrong. They possess no sense of irony," Letterman lamented. "They don't understand the wit, the intelligence, or the originality behind what he was doing."

Dave always admired the durability of Robin Williams. "I'm not one of those comedians who'll stay on as long as you let them," Letterman confessed. "Give Robin Williams five hours and he'll do five hours. Give me twenty minutes, and I'll say, 'Will you settle for fifteen?' "

But comedians were not the only celebrities Dave made observations about. He became interested in Rush Limbaugh during the 1992 presidential campaign. "I think, politics notwithstanding, [that] this guy is very entertaining. I've listened to his radio show. He's very calculated. He says and does thing to create an impression, to get a reaction. . . .

"I find him first and foremost a showman. His television show is just him sitting at a desk, telling you what he thinks. And for that to be entertaining for half an hour, whether you agree with him or not, is no small accomplishment."

Howard Stern struck him a bit differently. "I'll listen to him a lot for a while, and then I won't listen to him a lot for a while. Over the years, I've tried to figure out a satisfying evaluation of Howard. And I just can't. There are times when he seems bright and witty to me, I just think, 'Damn, this guy's blue-chip!' And then other times I think, 'How can a person possibly say this?'

"I listened one day when Howard was giving away pairs of movie tickets to the first five guys who'd come down to the station and expose themselves. And I thought, 'Oh, man—the movie company must be down on their knees giving thanks to God!' You can't buy PR like this—guys are in there taking their pants off! I mean, can you do that? Can you invite somebody in off the streets and have them undress for movie tickets?"

Like most talk-show hosts, Letterman visited most of his rivals on occasion, and in turn invited many of them to be guests on his own show. One he did not. That one was Arsenio Hall.

"I've heard that he thinks that I don't care for him," Letterman said. "I assume that he doesn't really *believe* that because we don't even know each other."

There had been some screwup in the scheduling. "As I understand it, I think he was under the impression that we didn't want him on the show, and the producer felt it was too close to the beginning of *his* show. And it was just a matter of—well, he's got his own show. But I don't think he dislikes me. I certainly don't dislike him. I mean, I really don't *know* him."

On the other hand, David Letterman and Jay Leno were constantly on each other's shows. Leno has said again and again that if he had not been for Letterman during those early years, he never would have gone on the *Tonight Show* at all. Leno was always the consummate comedian—he even watched the competition, especially *Late Night*.

"One night," he said, "I was watching the show, and Dave comes out and does this joke: 'It was raining today, and Dolly Parton was caught without an umbrella. But her shoes didn't get wet.' Now, I'm thinking, 'Gosh, that doesn't sound like a David Letterman joke to me,' when [Dave] says, 'Oh, wait a minute, hand me that cue card.' And he turns it over and says, 'Sorry, folks. That was left over from last year's Bob Hope special.'"

Letterman was always fascinated by big macho actors like Clint Eastwood. "I was on the *Tonight Show* with him . . . and I made some remark about his clothes. He dressed like, whatever came into Goodwill today—so I said, 'You! Mr. Movie Star! You could have worn a tie.' So Clint looks at me and says something like, 'Nice socks,' and gets a huge laugh.

"So I stand up and challenge him to a fight. I thought, 'This is *great*! Me, a 180-pound scared, wimpy ninny, and now I'm calling out Clint Eastwood on national television! Wouldn't it be great if he'd just stood up and dropped me? Boom! *There you go, funny boy!*'"

"He's so cool. I just loved *Unforgiven*. Especially the end: he kills, like, seven thousand people, then moves to San Francisco to open a grocery store, as if to say, 'Let's just leave this unpleasantness behind.'"

Other film stars did not affect him the way Eastwood did. He was listening to Tom Hanks one night go on and on about how much he loved making a picture called *Joe Versus the Volcano*. It became obvious that the thing was a bomb, but Letterman just kept nodding and smiling. Finally, he had reached the end of his endurance. And he came up with a question that was most charitable in the instance.

"Tom," he said, leaning forward as if vitally interested, "what's the deal with your hair?"

David Letterman was once asked how he would feel if Regis Philbin turned out to be a smash hit. Telling someone the story later on, Letterman said, "I thought, 'What if this son of a bitch—' I know him and have a lot of respect for him— but 'What if he *was* successful?' It was just a fleeting moment, because I hope he is. After you've been through this crap once, it's impossible to wish anybody else in television ill."

They were searching for people to be on the show and the name of Tom Landry, the then coach of the Dallas Cowboys football team, came up. When Landry was approached to "appear on Letterman," he frowned in puzzlement. "Gosh, I don't know what it is," he said. It was explained to him in detail that Letterman was a late-night talk-show host. Landry thought about it for bit, and then frowned. "I'm not sure what I'll do."

N.B.: He did not appear.

Margot Kidder was worried about the time she was invited by Letterman's staff to plug a film she had made. "The first time on the show I was more than a little tense," she said, "and I held back. The second time I got smart and decided that I was just going to be silly. Now the show is fun to do."

When Mickey Rooney was talking about what he watched on television for *TV Guide* he said he didn't like any network shows at all. "I don't want to sound hypercritical, but they insult me with bad writing and laugh tracks." He added, "Telling me Candice Bergen is funny [in *Murphy Brown*] is like telling me Waterman is funny." Waterman? Did he mean Letterman? "Letterman! That's like telling me David Letterman is funny. . . Give me a break!"

Another Rooney named Andy didn't swoon at Letterman's humor, either. In fact, exactly the opposite. For some reason he and Letterman never did hit it off. Letterman said, "I get intimidated real easily by people. . . I remember our second or third show [when] we had Andy Rooney on from *60 Minutes*. I had always been a great admirer of Andy Rooney's, to the extent that I would get videotape copies of television programs he had put together because I thought he was doing some terrific work in the line of documentaries. We had him on and he intimidated me, and it just went from bad to worse and got ugly and just stupid after that."

Letterman was also somewhat uneasy the night he had on G. Gordon Liddy, the Watergate break-in figure. Dave did his usual quip when he introduced Liddy by describing him as "an author and convicted felon—an introduction we don't use too often."

Liddy started out plugging his current lecture tour. He was sharing the circuit with Timothy Leary, the Yale professor who had turned drug guru during the sixties. Ironically, Leary had once been arrested by Liddy when Liddy was a law-enforcement official prior to his Watergate days.

In an unsigned review in the *New York Times*, the writer described the interview as a conversation in which "the snidely arrogant Mr. Liddy began to take a clearly patronizing attitude toward an increasingly bristling Mr. Letterman. Johnny Carson," the writer claimed, "would have demolished this kind of guest with a single quip." Not so Letterman.

As the interview ended, Letterman asked Liddy what the future might hold for him.

Liddy: "The same as for you in the grand scheme of things—we shall provide a diet for the worms."

And thus Liddy succeeded in shooting himself in the foot without any help from Letterman.

When Joan Rivers left her enviable spot as permanent guest host for Johnny Carson on the *Tonight Show*, she moved to the new Fox network. This annoyed Carson no end. Even Letterman had something to say about Rivers.

"I think one thing you can't do in show business is burn bridges behind you. Show business is such an odd, quirky thing that you can be sued for several million dollars one day and then the next day the same company hires you to go to work for them. I think show business may be the one area where burning bridges doesn't mean anything."

But he had more to say. "I don't think anybody begrudges her making a move for success on her own terms. I just think she handled it in a graceless fashion." How? "By suddenly turning on NBC and saying unpleasant things about Johnny and the *Tonight Show*. I think there were going to be hard feelings regardless of how she handled it. But if it were me, I certainly would have tried to avoid things to generate ill feelings."

There was even a Letterman connection with Bill Clinton before he became President of the United States. In an indirect way, Letterman managed to alienate even the man who would eventually run the country.

"I can remember early on—right after Clinton did the *60 Minutes* thing—I was talking to Tom Shales [of the *Washington Post*] and, off the record, he asked, 'What do you think of Clinton?' "

Letterman had Clinton all figured out. "The guy's a pretender," he told Shales. "He doesn't have a chance in hell. This guy, he's not a President."

And his estimate of Clinton appeared in the *Washington Post* two days later. "My assessment of Clinton . . . completely [wrote] him off as a loser without fiber," Letterman said. "[Now] he's the *pars-dent*. So I know I'm going to pay for this. I know something ugly will happen, and he'll be behind it. Some huge tax audit, or he'll start nosing around my domestic staff."

In "An Open Letter to David Letterman," *Newsday*'s Terry Kelleher composed an epistle of hope—hope that when Letterman's show moved from 12:30 to 11:35 he would keep himself and his attitude as sharp and knowing as it was when he had interviewed Sharon Stone:

"Remember how the *Sliver* star came on all phony-sexy, then resisted your attempts to elicit something genuinely amusing?" Kelleher wrote to Letterman. "Remember your remark to Paul Shaffer when that dead-end conversation was over? 'Ah,' you said with a wave of the hand, 'who cares?' That's the Dave we want to see at 11:35. America can handle a premidnight snack that's not sugar coated."

CHAPTER TWELVE
The Uninvited

On May 22, 1988, a pleasant-looking woman in her midthirties drove up to the tollbooth on the New Jersey side of the Lincoln Tunnel. Beside her sat a three-year-old boy.

"Three dollars," announced the toll collector.

The woman smiled and shrugged her shoulders. "I don't have three dollars."

The toll collector surveyed the seventy-thousand-dollar midnight-blue Porsche Carrera she was driving and gave her a somewhat lopsided grin. "Oh, sure."

"I don't have it. But I'm sure you'll let me drive into New York."

"Oh?" said the by-now skeptical and curious toll taker.

"I'm Mrs. David Letterman and this is David, Jr.," the woman said, turning to the boy at her side.

"Uh huh," said the toll collector.

"Don't you think David Letterman is good for the toll?"

By this time the collector, who had heard a lot of stories about why drivers didn't have the proper toll, had decided that this time he was dealing with a certifiable patron. He called the Hudson County police, in whose jurisdiction he operated.

When they arrived, the woman went over her story once

again. When they asked her to prove that she was Mrs. David Letterman, she gave them permission to go through the glove compartment of the 1988 car.

There they found that the Porsche was indeed registered to David Letterman. But the woman who claimed to be Mrs. David Letterman could produce no proof as to her own identity. She was arrested and the police immediately contacted David Letterman's office at NBC studios in New York.

Letterman was in California at the time, they were told. Naturally, the Letterman office confirmed what the authorities already knew: that David Letterman was *not* married. Eventually, when he was finally contacted, he told them that he had given no one permission to drive his car.

Then Letterman telephoned the New Canaan Police Department and told them the story. The Hudson County police charged the woman who said she was Mrs. Letterman with "receiving stolen property"—that is, the car. By this time they had found out that her name was Margaret Ray, although she said she preferred to be called Mary Ray. But that was better than her initial statement—that her name was Jane Doe— which did not amuse the Hudson County police at all.

By now the story was developing further ramifications. New Canaan police visited the home of David Letterman and discovered that someone had forced open one of the front windows and broken into the house. In the garage, of course, there was no sign of Letterman's Porsche.

By now the officials in Hudson County had uncovered some more facts. The woman's real name was Margaret M. Ray. While she was detained there, she was separated from the boy who had been with her. His name, she finally admitted, was Alexander Ray. Her son was given into the custody of the New Jersey Division of Youth and Family Service.

Further investigation of Letterman's house in New Canaan revealed that someone had been living there. For example, detectives found that some of the plants had been watered and moved from one place to another. Also, a rug seemed to have been relocated in a like manner.

Captain Michael Angelastro of the New Canaan police observed: "It appears that someone has been living in the house for the last couple of days. We're not saying it was her," he said, referring to Margaret Ray. "We are not pursuing it."

Meanwhile, David Letterman declined to press charges. His reluctance to prosecute stemmed from the fact that he did not want the kind of attention such an action would attract to him in public.

And so all charges were dropped against Margaret Ray. Letterman's Porsche was returned to his garage by the New Canaan police and the house inspected once again. It seemed that everything would blow over and there would be no further problems relating to Letterman's uninvited guest.

Five days later—on May 27—a cabdriver picked up a woman at the New Canaan station of the New Haven Railroad and drove her out to the Letterman house, where she told him she was working as a housekeeper. When he turned to collect her fare of $7.50, she said she did not have a cent on her, but that she would get some money from the house.

As the cabdriver furtively watched her through the flowering bushes, she climbed in a window at the front of the house and returned a few minutes later with two dollars' worth of pennies. She said she would give him the rest when Mr. Letterman returned. The cabdriver agreed, drove off, and immediately telephoned the New Canaan police.

When the police arrived, they found the woman sitting in the living room of the Letterman house eating canned pineapple and leafing through magazines. A pile of clippings from other magazines was on the table next to her.

She told the police she was a housekeeper that David Letterman had hired to take care of his house in his absence.

"She was living there, from all indications, for a day or so," Michael McEnaney, a New Canaan police officer, said.

She could produce no proof of being Letterman's housekeeper. McEnaney said he would have to take her down to the station to clear things up. She refused to go.

"David wouldn't want to come home to anything but a clean house!" she told him indignantly.

A few phone calls cleared the air. Or, rather, fogged it up.

McEnaney arrested the woman, who finally admitted her name was Margaret Ray, and she was detained at the police station. Later, she was placed under twenty-five-thousand-dollar bail in Norwalk while she was to undergo psychiatric testing.

"What apparently happened," McEnaney said, "was [that] she was let out [of jail] in New Jersey, hopped a train, and came back into town."

Next day, New Canaan police got a warrant to charge her with two counts of burglary—for breaking into the house twice—and one count of larceny for allegedly stealing Letterman's sports car.

By now police investigators had located Margaret Ray's mother, a Mrs. Loretta DuVal of Greenwich, Connecticut. She informed them that her daughter had a history of mental problems, and had been traveling around the country on her own. She had been arrested several times before, but never for anything as serious as this.

And, interestingly enough, there had been a long court battle between Mrs. DuVal and Margaret Ray over custody of Alexander Ray, one of her sons. Alexander, at that point, was with his grandmother in Greenwich.

Actually, Margaret Ray had five children in all, and had been divorced from her husband for some time.

It was further discovered from people working for David Letterman at NBC that Margaret Ray had allegedly run up a number of luncheon and dinner tabs at restaurants around the Rockefeller Center area as Mrs. David Letterman.

The results of the psychiatric examination of Margaret Ray came through in June when Superior Court Judge James Bingham ruled after testimony from a doctor that she suffered from "impaired judgment."

According to Dr. James Alexander of Bridgeport, "She was rambling, exhibited flight of ideas, and was delusional. She feels there is a power of some kind controlling her behavior."

Judge Bingham then ordered her to be taken to a psychiatric hospital to be examined by a team of doctors to find out if she was fit to be tried in court.

A July hearing led Judge Bingham to order another test after the second psychiatrist, Dr. Sander H. Fogle of Fairfield Hills, told the court that he, too, believed she could not assist in her defense. He said she would be helped by psychotherapy and lithium treatments.

In September, she was released from the hospital and Norwalk Superior Court Judge Edward Levitt ordered her to give up all contact with David Letterman, except through the mail. She was told to return to her hometown of Crawford, Colorado.

She did so in October, according to her lawyer, Anita Cason. However, she soon returned to Connecticut to attend a custody hearing concerning her son Alexander, who was living with his grandmother in Greenwich.

Meanwhile, New Canaan police continued their watch at the Letterman house to make sure Margaret Ray did not try to return to her old pastime of breaking and entering, especially now that she was back in the area.

On February 24, 1989, the surveillance team saw a light inside Letterman's house, and, since he usually lived in an apartment in the city during the week, entered the house to see what was happening.

Wandering around the foyer of the Letterman place was Margaret Ray. This time she was allegedly found with marijuana in her possession, along with other drug equipment. She was arrested and charged with one felony count of first-degree trespass, and one misdemeanor count each of possession of marijuana and of drug paraphernalia.

She appeared in court on February 27, and was released on her own recognizance to appear for arraignment in Norwalk Superior Court on Friday.

However, that very night she was found again inside the Letterman house and arrested once more on a new charge of first-degree criminal trespass. Police had received a complaint about 2 A.M. on Tuesday morning that there was an unwanted person inside the house.

"I just wanted to pay him a surprise visit," Margaret Ray told police.

"She's getting to be a regular," said Patrolman Michael McEnaney. "We're on a first-name basis. Unfortunately, I don't think she's a well person."

She was imprisoned at Niantic State Prison in lieu of five thousand dollars bail, with a competency hearing scheduled for her on March 15, at which she was ordered to undergo further psychiatric tests even though one doctor—Dr. James Alexander—found her competent to testify.

Norwalk Superior Court Judge John Ryan ordered a three-member panel, consisting of a psychiatrist, a psychologist, and a social worker, to examine her at the Niantic State Prison.

As she entered the courthouse, she called out to reporters: "I'm ready to talk. I've had enough. I've seen enough."

She said that she wanted to have her son back. And, in spite of the warning of the judge not to make any statement on her own, she addressed him:

"I want to apologize to the court. I set myself up."

On April 5, she appeared before Superior Court Judge Harold H. Dean, who ruled her incompetent to assist in her defense.

"I wanted to plead guilty, but I wasn't given any credibility for that stance," Margaret Ray complained during the hearing.

The charges against her were now those of criminal trespassing, burglary, possession of marijuana, and larceny—the burglary an added charge, which was the result of being found wearing a wristwatch belonging to David Letterman.

Anita Cason, Ray's attorney, said that the wearing of the wristwatch did not mean she intended to steal it. She had put the watch on because she was attempting to clean Letterman's house and wanted to know how much time it took.

In the end, Judge Dean ordered her transferred from Niantic State Prison to Fairfield Hills Hospital in Newtown. The hospital staff was ordered to report on her condition every ninety days.

On May 30, Margaret Ray pleaded guilty to using Letterman's car without his permission, and to two counts of first-degree criminal trespass. Norwalk Superior Court Judge William F. Hickey, Jr., then sentenced her to a one-year suspended sentence and three years probation. He ordered her released from the state mental hospital, but as part of her probation, she had to stay away from Letterman and continue to undergo psychiatric treatment. All other charges against her were dropped.

On August 24, 1989, David Letterman was at home and saw Margaret Ray moving around the grounds of his house. He immediately called the New Canaan police, but said he would not press charges. However, her presence on the Letterman grounds violated the terms of her probation.

By the time he caught up with her, she was at the tennis court, raking leaves. He knew who she was even though he had never seen her before in person.

"I'd like a glass of water," she told Letterman.

Letterman threw up his hands. What kind of thing was this? Now she wanted water.

"Okay," he said. "Finish raking the yard, then I'll get your damn water."

He went inside, got her a drink of water, came out, and told her she had a half hour to get off the property.

"I hope you didn't call the police," she said.

"Margaret, I *did* call the police. You'd better get out of here."

She went ballistic, yelling and screaming at him. Letterman backed off. But she left the property. The police caught up with her at the New Canaan Railroad station and arrested her.

This was the fifth time in two years that she had been on Letterman's property uninvited. The court was not quite so lenient this time. Superior Court Judge Harold Dean gave her nine months in Niantic Women's Prison.

On the television show *A Current Affair* just before the trial, Margaret Ray said that she was in love with David Letterman, and that when she was in his house she busied herself by "writing, watching television, cleaning, washing the windows, and doing the floors. I like housework.

"I don't think there's another woman alive who could love David Letterman as much as I do. He's the dominant figure in my life."

She said she had become infatuated with him after seeing him on a documentary program. "I could tell you that it was love at first sight."

At one point she said, "I went [to his house] to give him a notebook. . . . I talked to him and he was in a bad mood."

She served seven months of the nine-month term and then she was released. Meanwhile, Letterman returned from a trip to the West Coast. It was around two o'clock in the morning.

"There was an immediate sense of something not right," Letterman recalled. "Things had been moved in a way that you would never move your own belongings. The kitchen sink was full of dirty dishes. So I realized that somebody was in the house." He could see that there was a window ajar in a downstairs room.

Letterman called the New Canaan police. The police came and he watched as they went from one room to another turning on lights.

"They finally found her asleep upstairs in bed and bounced her," Letterman related. He did not choose to press charges, and she was released. She left peaceably.

"The incident that was most frightening came a week later." Letterman was in bed. Suddenly, he thought he smelled smoke, which was "not a good sign." "So I sat up in bed, and at the end of the hallway I could determine the silhouette of the woman standing there. That scared me. It scared me for a second, and then I realized: 'Oh, I know what this is. There's no trouble.' I rolled over and called the New Canaan police." She heard him on the phone, and ran out of the house.

Between 1988 and 1991, Margaret Ray trespassed on Letterman's property at least six times. In 1992, there were no such recurrences, and then on July 7, 1993, she appeared again.

"I'm camped out on your tennis court," she said in a note to Letterman.

Letterman thought it might be an old note, but later on, he decided to send for the police. When they went down to the court, they found she had been camped out there for three days. She was even doing her laundry in Letterman's swimming pool.

Meanwhile, a series of letters—at one time she was writing him every day—were changing in tone. In the summer of 1993, she seemed to be declaring that she was finished with David Letterman.

In August 1993, Norwalk State Superior Court Judge Edward Rodriguez, Jr., gave her a one-year suspended sentence, effective after she served four months in a correctional facility, for her appearance on the Letterman tennis court.

After she served her time, she would be on probation for two years, during which period she would not be allowed to contact Letterman directly or indirectly, nor should she enter New Canaan as long as Letterman lived there.

Judge Rodriguez asked her if she understood the proceedings.

"Mr. Letterman did know I was coming," she said. "He did not respond to letters I had sent him. I think that celebrities should answer their mail."

He reprimanded her when she told him, "I'll write letters," and added, "People have a right to peace in their own homes." Referring to a passage in a letter dated August 20 to David Letterman, he said: "I'm looking forward to that presentation you made in your August 20 letter, that you and David Letterman are through."

Letterman had profound compassion for his uninvited guest. "She is a woman who spends her days in deep confusion," he said. "She is a woman who knows few moments of lucidity or reality. She is a troubled woman who suffers great free-floating anxiety and is better when she's medicated, but not much."

He shrugged.

"This woman is no more to me than a nuisance; she's not a threat."

CHAPTER THIRTEEN
Dave on Dave

"I can't sing, dance, or act. What else would I be but a talk-show host?"

Although Dave Letterman's amusing self-assessment might read more like a one-liner from one of his nightly openers than a true appraisal of his worth, it pretty much represented what in some ways he always thought about himself.

One thing about David Letterman. Of all the talk-show hosts, he came into the business, quite likely, with the least admiration for his own sense of comedy. Yes, he loved to make people laugh. But just as much, he loved to make them writhe. He was always the consummate kidder—a kind of Mark Twain in jeans and T-shirt.

His aspiration was always to keep his vision clear, force his mind to unclutter itself of day-to-day fads, and keep steady aim on the distant horizon where truth and vision lurked just beyond the rim.

"You probably do have to change and grow," he conceded once. "If you don't, one of two things may happen. Either you'll dry up and blow away, or, in twenty years, the great cycle of show business will come around again, and you'll be like the *Monkees*—right back on television!"

The *Monkees*, incidentally, was a youth-oriented comedy sitcom starring a Beatles lookalike singing group in the sixties. The show ran from September 1966 through August 1968. The point of Letterman's statement concerned a later attempt in 1987 to reprise the series with new actors—but the revival only lasted for thirteen episodes.

Unlike most of his fellow comics who became talk-show hosts, David Letterman was always able to see himself quite clearly and to understand exactly where he fit into the milieu of television entertainment. He never had any false visions of his own abilities and talents. If anything, he saw himself as much less a celebrity than he was in actuality. His words frequently tended to a low-key type of British understatement. Many of his laughs came from this sharp, realistic perception of his own shortcomings.

He not only understood himself and his place in the entertainment firmament, but he understood the business itself, and was able to articulate his comprehension far better than most of his peers. He understood what he was doing for others—in the manner of entertaining them—and what he was doing for himself when he performed. And he frequently discussed these points in public.

"I'm just the happiest, the best I ever feel, from five-thirty to six-thirty," he told *Gentleman's Quarterly* in 1990 as he reviewed his career on late-night television. Those hours were the hours in which he taped his show to be broadcast later that night. "All this other stuff is tough for me—personnel problems, people who are unhappy because they are in an office with one window as opposed to two. I didn't go into this [business] because I am a personnel expert."

One of his weaknesses had always been his relationships with the many, many people who were dependent on him for a livelihood. He did not make any great effort to socialize with those he knew peripherally or even intimately. His eye was always on the finished product—the show he was performing in. Between scenes, when the commercials were whirring through the broadcast heavens, he frequently looked down at his notes and did not chat amiably with his guest or guests as he might be imagined to do. Yet when he appeared again, it seemed that no connection had been broken between guest and host.

No, he did not go into the business to please others around him, or even to have long and happily extended relationships with them. He went into it for one reason only.

"I think most comics are the happiest they ever are when they're onstage and things are working well for them, because then they're being reinforced for something very, very personal. It represents an acceptance the likes of which you'll never get anywhere else."

He understood the rush he got when he was out there in front of the crowd. He knew what it did internally for him. He never apologized to anyone for *liking* the feeling of power it gave him. But he sometimes understood how it affected those around him who were not in the target of millions of eyes.

"I always feel a little guilty because I'm the one who gets to go out there and for a few minutes I'm the focus of all the attention of those people. It's not the assistant director, associate producer. It's not the head writer. It's *me*. And I'm telling you, even if that's synthetic, the *feeling* of the response of those people just makes you."

Later, he expanded on that feeling of response and connectedness.

"It's like being injected with a huge dose of morphine and you just think, 'Oh, man!' It really gets your attention. It can be a very emotional thing."

Emotional—but intellectual, as well. And he knew what he owed the people who were watching him, as well as what his guests owed them.

In *TV Guide* in 1993 he said, "When you come out to be on a show, it 's not an homage, it's not a newspaper interview. You're there to show people *why* they ought to spend seven and a half bucks for your new movie, or watch your show on TV. Even I did it: When I'd go on the *Tonight Show*, I'd spend weeks writing anecdotes, working on stories. It's not easy. And it's not fun. But it's what is important. You owe it to the people watching."

And there was always the satisfaction of knowing that he was successful in entertaining people.

"When I was first starting out, my real dream was to work at a radio station in Cincinnati. Did I want a network television show? Sure. But the truth of it is, it's the same circumstances working for Channel 13 in Indianapolis as it is for CBS in New York. It's the same equipment, the same techniques—and you get the same satisfaction from doing a good job. That's what's important."

Letterman's analyses of the various types of shows in the television industry always had a textbook simplicity about them and exhibited a definite clarity of vision. For example, in *Esquire* in 1986:

"The deal with a talk show is, it doesn't have to be stupendous. It's not great, it's not bad, it just goes by. It sticks to the videotape. It lights up the screen. Actors come on repeating the same clichés they say on every other talk show, but it doesn't matter. These things are really easy to do. They're dirt cheap. You build a set once, pay everybody as little as you can, and the guests all come on for scale. If a talk show is even moderately successful, you can nurse it along for a few years with very little expense."

He then pointed out the ways in which a talk show resembled a game show—not particularly in the presentation, but in the *financing*. To stimulate the quick buck in TV, the two most visible and successful genres of shows were the game show and the talk show. "If you come up with a *Wheel of Fortune*—good Lord, that thing makes more money than General Motors, doesn't it? It just *churns* out the dough."

And Letterman did understand the magic of the talk show— that is, the *reason* for its continuing success. "There's something reassuring about it. I guess it's roughly comparable to putting an alarm clock in a basketful of puppies. So you have all those people sitting around in suits and talking about their careers. And for some reason you don't want them to say anything novel or different. You want to hear them say what other actors and actresses have said over the years on other talk shows."

Letterman had always been more than honest about his own talent—or, as he considered it—his lack of it.

"I don't think I was a good stand-up comedian," he told *Time* magazine. "I could do the job. I learned the skills of making a roomful of drunks laugh. But I never really *enjoyed* it. I always felt like I was not enough. To me, when you go see a comic, you want to . . . see lights and props and balloons and fruit being smashed. You want to see something because you're spending something like twenty to twenty-five bucks. They came to see me, and all I really had was thirty minutes of jokes."

And comedy was always changing, especially on television. He explained to Tom Shales what he meant in fuller detail in a *Washington Post* story: "Before, a stand-up comic or an observational humorist had the entire horizon from which to draw comedy. Now you get people who have been raised on television and their source of comedy is nothing *but* television. And I think that may be a little limiting. And I do that. My stand-up act was mostly, 'Did you see this on television; it was so stupid, wasn't it?' And it was funny because there are millions and millions of people who went through the same process. But I don't know that it's the best approach in the long run."

He had always admitted that he might appear cranky and annoyed in front of the camera—but he continued to maintain that that particular expression really meant something else. It was, he claimed, an antidote for the kind of smarmy euphoria so prevalent on the air.

"You see so much happiness and so much phony effervescence and so much manufactured joy on television. In fact, this is something Jack Paar told me a long time ago: 'It's okay to let people know you're upset, or pretend you're upset, because then, if they're sitting at home, they say, "Jeez, I wonder if he really is upset!" ' And I've always kind of felt that there was a certain amount of truth in that."

Letterman understood that his lack of talent extended further than just his inability to be a stand-up comic. "I was intimidated by guests. So it took a while to overcome that. I remember at one point having a major shift of attitude. After two or three years, it didn't seem that we could do anything to improve the [show's] ratings. I can remember just feeling this frustration and despair and exhaustion, and it was kind of like—screw it. At that point I think I was able to relax more."

In the early days, Letterman did not know quite where the show was headed—up or down. Nor did he really know clearly what kind of show it was, as he told the *Los Angeles Times*:

"There was a time, the first three or four years of the show, when we were described as a cult show, as a real college kind of show. And in those days, I was grateful for any audience. But I thought to myself, 'If this is true, how am I going to feel when I'm in my forties, doing a show for eighteen-year-old kids who are sneaking beer into the dorm?'

"You know? And I guess, more importantly, [I thought], 'How are they going to feel about me?' But I don't think you can plot. I don't think you can predict what you're going to do. I think you just have to sort of evolve and grow the way you would if you were running a hardware store. And people will either keep coming in to buy wrenches, or they won't."

Because he had always depended on his ability to make fun of people from his earliest days on earth, he realized as he matured that he might be hurting the very people he wanted to help—and turning off an audience that he wanted to turn *on*.

"It used to trouble me that people thought our sole purpose for being in business was to make fun of people. Unfortunately, there is no joke that does not make fun of somebody. I try to make me [the butt of the joke], as often as not, or the show, or somebody in our little group. So if we do say something that looks like we're making fun of somebody else, it's in the spirit of everything. But some people don't buy that. I know that some people can't stand me, and it troubles me because I think we're just trying to do the funniest show we know how."

Letterman had always recognized the fact that he must be exactly what he appeared to be in order to be the proper host of his talk show. "I think when you do a show like this night after night, you're going to have to be a bigger version of the person you actually are. And you're going to react more strongly to things that you would not react so strongly to in your own life. I like to think it's kind of an honest representation of the person I am."

It has been said that David Letterman was always the most borrowed-from performer on television. As Tom Shales put it, "His put-down sensibility now permeates the culture. A compliment! It makes him squirm."

But Letterman had a rejoinder to Shales's observation. "If that's true, it's only because I have borrowed from a lot of guys who came before me. I mean, if it were true, if we could prove it, then I think I'd be flattered by it, but I'm not so self-absorbed that I think there is a lot of truth to it."

He never liked to reveal too much of the real David Letterman on the air, although he had created a persona that portrayed sincerity, honesty, and integrity.

"I like talking about things that happen in my life, if I think I can make me the butt of the joke. But I'm not crazy about actually talking about real things in my life: the women in my life, or my own political feelings and beliefs, limited as they are. If something funny happens in the supermarket, I like trying to talk about that. Because I think—and this may be completely misguided—if I were at home watching a show, I'd like to hear about Johnny Carson's getting a flat tire."

And he concluded: "But I don't want to start explaining in great detail what makes me happy, what makes me sad, that kind of crap."

In 1986, when Letterman's *Late Show* ratings suddenly began to rise in a modest but very real way and the show was termed by the communications pundits a "success," Dave did not allow himself to be escalated to the moon by the numbers he was shown.

"We worked long and hard the first two or three years [of *Late Night*], and we did the same show that we're doing now, and yet the ratings are getting better, and none of us knows specifically why. I just don't trust it. And why should I, given the vagaries of television? There's no great satisfaction in suc-

ceeding in television. What good is it? CBS could come along
with a new package of action shows and knock us right to
hell. It's not much of an accomplishment really. That's why
we try to take it in stride."

He was philosophical about whatever might happen. "The
more successful you are, the more similarity you have, and
the quicker people will tire of it. I hope they don't . . . I think
maybe what's happened is we've just kind of worn people
down. So they say, 'Oh, all right, Christ, we'll watch your
damn show.' "

David Letterman once denied that he was really a talk-show
host in real life. What he said was this:

"I'm not a talk-show host, but I play one on TV."

And that about summed it up.

CHAPTER FOURTEEN
Head-Hunting

Some hairline cracks were beginning to show in the relationship between David Letterman and NBC even before the big break that resulted from the selection of Jay Leno over the host of *Late Night* as Johnny Carson's replacement.

The principal annoyance had to do with NBC's deal with Arts & Entertainment, a cable network that consisted mainly of syndicated material, usually in rerun form. What NBC did was license *all* of David Letterman's shows—owned lock, stock, and barrel by NBC—to A & E for showing whenever they wanted.

This meant that Letterman might be competing with himself any time he went on the air. There was more to it than competition. Too much Letterman was even worse than not enough Letterman. Saturation—called "overexposure" in the entertainment business—could kill just as surely as underexposure.

With typical midwestern taciturnity, Letterman did not rush into the NBC offices and berate everyone in sight. But his muttering was heard. Little attention was paid to it. The deal had already been set. Moves that made profits for the network were not questioned unless someone in the power structure made an issue of them.

But Letterman was simmering beneath the surface all the same. And that postponed the moment of truth that would occur between him and NBC to May 1991, when critical mass would be reached and the bomb would burst.

Actually, there were tremors even before May. On February 11, 1991, the *New York Post* printed a story with the bold headline:

THERE GOES JOHNNY!

To explain the somewhat ambiguous headline, the subhead read: "NBC Looking to Dump Carson for Jay Leno." The gist of the story was that NBC wanted Carson out so that they could replace him with Jay Leno, since they thought Leno could draw "a younger audience more attractive to advertisers."

Nowhere in the story did the name of David Letterman appear. And yet it had been known in the industry for years that Letterman fully expected to be the replacement when Johnny Carson decided to hang up his spurs. After all, he was the logical one to fill the spot since he followed Carson every night and had professional links to him, inasmuch as *Late Night* was coproduced by Carson's company.

Letterman had spoken often about the idea of taking over the *Tonight Show*. "In the back of my mind, if I weren't asked some day to do it, I'd feel kind of sad. Yet, doing it—that's my worst nightmare. That I'd be foolish enough to take the Carson position if offered to me, that I'd die a miserable death in that time slot, and meanwhile NBC had given my old show to someone who was quite happy to keep doing it." After a pause, he went on. "Maybe the prudent thing would be to let some other poor bastard walk into the fray for several months, and then try doing the show [myself]."

And now, apparently, that second contingency seemed the only possibility for him. Sure enough, on May 23, 1991, Johnny Carson appeared at a press conference at Carnegie Hall and told the world that May 22, 1992, would be his last night on the *Tonight Show*. Soon enough, NBC announced that he would be replaced by Jay Leno, just as had been predicted in the February 1991 news leak.

When Letterman heard the news, the press reported immediately that he was "fit to be tied." Somehow that did not sit right with the Letterman persona, which, if not always dignified, was at least more or or less low profile.

"I've never been tied in my life," he said with a smile, turning the word into a typical double entendre. "There's not a man alive who can tie me!"

But he did admit that if the *Tonight Show* had been offered him, he would have taken it.

Warren Littlefield, the president of NBC Entertainment, was quoted in a press release. "Leno has proven extremely popular with the late-night audience, and we are confident that the show will continue its late-night dominance for many, many years."

Letterman's champion at NBC had been Brandon Tartikoff, but for some reason Littlefield never seemed to warm up to the *Late Night* host the way Tartikoff had. And the negative feeling between the two men was mutual.

What *really* incensed Letterman was the *way* in which NBC had chosen to deliver the bad news. Robert Wright, president of NBC, who sat in an office not too many steps from Letterman's, did not take part at all in the act itself. Instead, he telephoned Warren Littlefield and John Agoglia *in Los Angeles* and instructed them to fly east and tell Letterman what the network had decided.

That put the frosting on the cake for Letterman!

As for Leno, he pretended to know nothing about Letterman's interest in the *Tonight Show* job. "This is not a case of any sort of struggle going on," he said. "I've just been sitting in the wings, and when Johnny said he wanted to go, great! They called me, and I said, 'Yeah, fine, let's do it.' This isn't some sort of competition or power-struggle thing.

"I must admit I did not have a clue till it hit the papers that Dave had designs on the job. I never heard it mentioned. It was never brought up."

On August 30, 1991, David Letterman appeared on the

Johnny Carson *Tonight Show*. And he came prepared to have the final word.

As he referred to David Letterman's feelings about the choice of Jay Leno to host *Tonight*, Carson looked his guest in the eye.

"Just how pissed off are you?" he asked with a smile.

Letterman let the reaction of the audience subside before he answered.

"You keep using language like that and you're going to find yourself out of a job," he warned Carson.

Carson nodded. "There were rumors you were going to bomb NBC," he said.

Letterman smiled faintly. "I hate waiting in line." Then he went into his obviously prepared statement as if to confirm his carefully structured laid-back persona. "I'm not angry. I'm not angry at NBC about this. I'm not angry at Jay Leno about this. I'm not angry at you or the *Tonight Show* about this.

"Now if the network had come to me and said, 'Dave, we want you to have this show,' then a week later they said, 'Dave, we don't want you to have this show,' *then* I would have been angry. But I have a show and NBC can do whatever it wants to with this show. Now, would I *like* to have this show? Oh sure—yeah."

It was not the final word. Later on, Letterman had one more remark to make about the situation.

"Before we continue, I think we should congratulate our friend Jay Leno for being selected as the host of the *Tonight Show*. And the good news for *us* is, *we* get *Stump the Band*."

But the harmony and good nature that oozed out of Letterman on the Carson show was only a cosmetic for the public role he had chosen to play. Privately, he was seething. And what he *did* during those weeks and months finally demonstrated how he felt about NBC and the way they had treated him.

The first thing that happened was the result of some past actions that had apparently irritated Letterman in his dealings with his longtime manager, Jack Rollins. Whatever the problem was, or problems were, the two parted company after twelve years of association in May. Rollins let it be known that he had simply retired. Rumors said that Letterman wanted more muscle in his upcoming negotiations.

The next step was an obvious one. Letterman went shopping for a new agent. Helped by Peter Lassally, now Letterman's coexecutive producer, he found him in Michael Ovitz, a power broker well known in Hollywood circles, and a member of the formidable Creative Artists Agency.

There seemed to be no question but that Letterman wanted to make a change—and it would be an earth-shaking one. At least within the confines of the entertainment business.

It did not take long for word to get around. The snap of a thumb, if that. Almost immediately, people began to buddy up to Letterman. Big people. Important people.

King World, the syndicator of *Wheel of Fortune* and *The Oprah Winfrey Show*, began to make interesting comments to him.

Fox Broadcasting, trying to make a fourth at the three-handed game of Television Network, sent him a batting cage for his birthday. They also began talking about an eleven o'clock show. They even had an idea to perform a blockbusting evening lineup: teaming Letterman up with Chevy Chase in a one-two late-night punch.

Paramount and ABC were most interested in Letterman, but they were more or less committed to *Nightline*, their big 11:30 show that was running even the *Tonight Show* a very good race, and beating it out on some *big* news days.

Viacom, which owned several cable networks like MTV, VH-1, and Nickelodeon, came up with some lucrative bids and some vague ideas about a new show for Letterman.

And that put NBC squarely behind the eight ball. The network had already made its decision and hired Leno. Leno's contract had a ten-million-dollar clause in it, which would give Leno that amount if NBC defaulted on their contract with him. If they caved in and gave Letterman the *Tonight Show*, NBC would have to eat the ten-million-dollar default that would go to Leno.

CBS?

CBS had everything to gain and nothing to lose.

Ovitz was having a field day. How could he lose? He suspected that Letterman was even more charismatic than NBC and his fans had thought. At a different time, he might even be a blockbuster personality. He *had* matured. At least, some. And the old edge was still there—the edge that had always served him well with most people.

And it was at CBS that serious considerations were being discussed by serious men at serious late-night meetings. Howard Stringer was president of CBS, and it was he who had the dream of moving Letterman into CBS's 11:30 P.M. spot—a spot that had always been filled with what Letterman once called "Freeze-Dried Movies," action-adventure series, and other vacuous crud.

What if—?

Howard Stringer made his first approach to Letterman in April at an awards ceremony, and that began a continuous conversation between the two men. But Stringer, who was a strategist as well as a most ingratiating talker, did not confine his target to Letterman. Instead, he developed a three-pronged attack.

Not only did he begin taking Letterman out to expensive restaurants in New York, in the Hamptons, and in Los Angeles and its suburbs, but began to move in on Letterman's long-time intimate, Bob Morton, and Peter Lassally.

He had discovered through judiciously sounding out people in the broadcasting industry that indeed David Letterman *was* "pissed off" at NBC—to a degree that no one had really suspected inside Rockefeller Center. And so he began working his wiles.

With Letterman, Stringer knew exactly what he had to do. "It was Howard's job to *humanize* CBS," one insider said. "He's from the same generation. He appreciates irreverence. He basically told [Letterman], 'I'm your biggest fan. I live to watch your show.'"

That was easy to take after all the ridiculousness at NBC. Letterman began to *like* Stringer. And so Ovitz got to work. By November 1992, he opened up bids for a David Letterman

show. He had hammered out six main points—critical issues—
that Letterman wanted.

They included the following:

- Salary: $14 million a year.
- The 11:30 P.M. time slot.
- Access to a nationwide audience.
- A multiyear commitment.
- Ownership of the program.
- A percentage of the profits from whatever show *followed* the Letterman show.

The inclusion of the "ownership of the program" clause was
a direct result of NBC's leasing of all those early Letterman
shows that the network owned and Letterman did not.

There were offers all around.

Only two bids were viable ones. One was from Viacom, the
syndicator. But because it was not a network, it simply could
not guarantee the size of the audience it could deliver.

In the end, it was CBS that Letterman was most interested
in. But was CBS really interested in him? The answer was
yes. Definitely. Their offer was a beaut.

News leaks appeared like clockwork in the media. In September 1992, a story appeared in the Bible of the broadcasting
industry—*Variety*—to the effect that Letterman was unhappy
with his work at NBC and might opt out during his next
contract talks with the network.

"There have been a lot of friendly lunches going on" regarding Letterman's future, the story said.

But NBC's publicist, Rosemary Keenan, said renewal talks
were continuing, since Letterman had been "a valued member
of the NBC family for the past ten years and it is our hope
to have him stay at NBC beyond his current contract."

The words "hope" and "current" were the loophole words—
just in case he flew the coop.

Long before this, the legal department at NBC had indulged itself in late-night sessions of their own. It was obvious
that if Letterman did indeed leave NBC—and it seemed

highly likely at that point, in spite of all the ongoing PR clap-trap—he would be taking away a show that was one of NBC's biggest money makers. And so the best thing in the world to do would be to throw roadblocks in the way of Letterman.

Pawing through the pages of its contract with Letterman, the courtroom sharpies came up with a great idea. Since NBC owned the show, it virtually owned almost everything Letterman had *done* on the show. Letterman was an employee. What an employee did in a firm belonged to the firm.

Word went out. NBC was claiming proprietorship of such Letterman trademarks as Stupid Pet Tricks, Top Ten Lists, and even the World's Most Dangerous Band, the nomenclature of Paul Shaffer's studio group.

As for Larry (Bud) Melman, he, too, belonged to NBC.

The lawyers called all these items "intellectual properties" of NBC.

It was no joke. CBS's lawyers knew that. There were indeed "intellectual properties" that Letterman could not take with him if he walked. Where would the line be drawn?

"I don't foresee any specific changes at this time," Letterman said. "One of two things will happen. We'll just do all of the stuff that we want to do, and that'll be fine. [Or] we'll do all the stuff we want to do and they'll sue us, and, you know, that'll be fine. And by the way, if that comes to trial, get a seat down front!"

This brouhaha prompted Jay Leno to use the idea in one of his stand-ups. He dreamed up a fictitious "NBC memo" about what David Letterman could use and what he could *not* use from his NBC show if he went somewhere else.

"Guests on Letterman's [new] show may not sit down. The idea originated with Steve Allen. Therefore, all Letterman guests must either stand or squat.

"Letterman may not throw a pencil through a window. Nor may he use an incendiary device to blow up a GM pickup truck. Those are both intellectual properties of NBC.

"Letterman may no longer make fun of 'pinhead network executives.' Pinhead network executives are the exclusive property of NBC."

On October 30, 1992, it was announced that David Letterman was negotiating for rival offers in exchange for a three-month extension of his current NBC contract. That meant that he would broadcast at least up through late June 1993 on NBC.

In the end, it was not a hard decision for Letterman to make, all things considered. He had left NBC a long time ago, in spirit, if not in the flesh.

On December 8, the other shoe dropped. On that day, David Letterman informed NBC that he had accepted an offer from CBS to host a talk show on that network opposite the *Tonight Show* on NBC. NBC had until January 15, 1993, to match the CBS offer of from $14 to $16 million.

In the end, NBC came through with the big one. They would give Letterman the *Tonight Show* after Jay Leno had run out his contract. The catch was that Letterman would have to wait seventeen months to take over—until May 1994.

He was torn. He phoned around. The conflicted advice he got only aggravated his own indecision. In the end he decided to walk.

As Bill Carter had it in *The Late Shift: Letterman, Leno and the Network Battle for the Night,* David's final call was to his mother in Indianapolis.

"NBC has offered me the *Tonight Show,* but I think I'm going to go to CBS."

A pause. "Well," she said, "I just hope you know what you're doing."

And so it was that at a press conference on January 14, 1993, David letterman announced officially that he was switching from NBC to CBS.

"I never dated Amy Fisher," he observed at the beginning of the press conference. "I fixed her car. I helped her with her homework. I never laid a hand on Amy Fisher."

Then he gave praise to his old network, NBC, for behaving honorably, and like gentlemen.

"What I *will* miss most are the back rubs from Irving R. Levine. The man is a master."

A reporter asked Letterman if he would continue any of his old bits, like Stupid Pet Tricks, on his new show at CBS.

"They own the rights to my old ice-dancing routine," Letterman sighed. Of course, Letterman had made it a point for years to say that he did not dance.

At the end of the press conference, Letterman was asked when he would begin at CBS.

"In August," he said. "And we should probably finish up around Labor Day." He turned quickly to CBS president Laurence Tisch, who was on the podium next to him. "That's a joke, Larry."

Letterman closed the press conference with a mention of Johnny Carson. He said he had talked to him on the phone a few days before.

"I don't know a person in comedy or television who didn't grow up with Johnny Carson as a role model. The man has been encouraging and helpful to me in ways that he doesn't know I know about."

Did Carson have any advice to give Letterman?

"Yes," Letterman responded. "He said, 'Stop calling me!' "

CHAPTER FIFTEEN
The New Dave

Once the date of David Letterman's first show on the CBS network was set—it would be August 30, 1993—CBS suited up its entire flack corps and ordered them to create sound bites and distribute public relations material everywhere to let the world know the news it already knew.

The new CBS show would be called *The Late Show with David Letterman*, which was at least not *exactly* the same as *Late Night with David Letterman*. Apparently the idea was to be just about the same without being strictly the same. Anyway, all the legal beagles at NBC knew that it was not possible to copyright a title. Theoretically Letterman could call his new show *Late Night* . . . but, then, he too, wanted something to indicate change.

Using *Late Show* echoed eerily the ill-fated late-night show Fox Network had initiated with Joan Rivers in 1988. But apparently CBS didn't care all that much. After all, if memory serves correct, CBS had called their rerun movies *The Late Show* some years before.

The hype for CBS's new *Late Show* was monumental. Sound bites featuring Letterman appeared in the middle of newscasts. They appeared in the midst of heartrending soap-opera scenes. They appeared at midnight, at 4 A.M., during breakfast. They appeared in the midst of horror movies.

No one could escape them.

A picture of Letterman would flash on the screen, and a voice-over would intone:

"Same Dave. Better time. New station."

There were, by actual count, as many as eighty commercials featuring Dave Letterman in typically caustic performances. They were created by his own writers in conjunction with CBS's in-house promotion department.

David Letterman, smiling: "Hey, I'm Dave and I want to be your television friend."

David Letterman, being charismatic: "Order now and receive a handsome tote bag."

David Letterman, leering: "If you remove the glass from the television set, you can feed me peanuts."

David Letterman, smirking: "Here's good news. We're saving the funny stuff."

In view of the hype and the intensity of the broadcasting of the sound bites, George F. Schweitzer, CBS's senior vice president of marketing and communications in New York, was underplaying it in typical laid-back Letterman fashion when he announced:

"Our strategy was not to overplay it. But there was a lot of attention we didn't expect, so it took on a life of its own. There was a line, but I don't think we stepped over it. Perhaps there was too much. If we could have tempered some of that, we should have."

Letterman himself played it cool but up front. With print competing with electronic in this media event, he appeared on the cover of *Time* magazine, and admitted that the campaign to plug his CBS debut was "officially embarrassing"— even to him.

Some of the commercials featured Letterman in a kind of smarmy attitude, opting for "cruel" over "cool."

Example: In one longer commercial, he mentioned the Ed Sullivan Theater, where the show would be broadcast from: "I'm going back to my live-theater roots. We'll get together with the kids from *Miss Saigon* and the kids from *Angels in America* and the kids from *Cats* and the kids from *My Sister Has Cramps* and we'll all have big theater parties and it'll be terrific; it'll be very exciting."

In another he said: "Thank you so very, very much for voluntarily bringing home a cassette full of commercials. I think it really, really takes a very, very special kind of person to do that."

The *New York Times* speculated that if the Letterman show on CBS was a success, the next morning's headline might well be:

LEO DUROCHER WAS RIGHT

But the promotion was not limited to the airwaves. It was everywhere. Letterman did his last show at NBC in the early part of summer, and proceeded to vanish from sight. But not totally.

He was keeping his eye on things that were happening, particularly at the Ed Sullivan Theater, which was being renovated for the new show.

"I've been in there three or four times, and every time I go in there, I stay in about eight minutes, and then all you see are big clouds of asbestos. And then I have to get out. I just think it might have been easier to renovate Ed Sullivan than the theater."

He even appeared a bit nostalgic about leaving NBC, where he had been for twelve years. "You know what happened? The Thursday night before the last night on the air, Bob Wright came up to the office and we sat and talked for about an hour. He gave me some very nice gifts, and I appreciated that. That meant a lot to me."

What gifts?

"Oh, a pack of gum."

He said he was treating his summer months as an extended vacation. Two months as against his usual time. It was, in effect, a vacation for himself and the job he did.

"I found that over the two months, I didn't say Butta-fuoco once."

Even so, he couldn't pass up a topicality or two. He talked about Mayor Dinkins and his move to give additional arms to the New York City police.

"It's about time they're armed as much as the kids in school."

He was asked if he was nervous about his move from one network to another and about his future with the new show.

"Maybe I'm just dumb, but I don't find myself in a cloud of anxiety about this. Of course, I'm full of gin."

Nor did he worry about tomorrow much.

"I'm not going to be around as long as Carson was around. After a period of time with this I will leave and go on. I'll probably never be on television again, on any kind of regular basis. This will be my new and final project." He paused. "You can hear America breathing a sigh of relief."

Would his audience change in his new fourteen-million-dollar-a-year time slot? Of course, *some* of the audience would change with the change in venue.

"Will they find a filthy-rich, almost prime-time Letterman less attractive than the familiar aw-shucks late-late-nighter? Perhaps. But if that happens, I'll just buy a new audience."

He pointed out that the new set at the Ed Sullivan Theater was much more ornate than his old one at NBC. "The reason for the larger desk," he confided, "is because Ed Sullivan is under there."

And the perks were terrific. "Now that I'm on CBS, I get to kill somebody on *Murder, She Wrote.*"

That brought up a question about violence on television. "I was out of the country when the networks announced this 'V' rating. Anyway, I heard this report about the number of acts of violence people watch. It's like, 'People are dead, people are dead, what's for lunch?' Does it *harm* people? I don't know, but I guess the rating is probably a pretty good thing. [My] new show, by the way, is going to be just as *violent* as we can make it!"

Would he remain in New York now that CBS was making

him a beautiful showcase for his program, or would he like living in California?

"Everyone likes living in California. You can't not like living in California. My problem with working in Los Angeles, whenever I get back there on vacation—I still own a home there—it's like a twenty-four-hour edition of *Entertainment Tonight*.

"You just can't escape show business. I like that when you leave the building here [in New York] you *don't* run into actors and producers, you run into people who are plumbers and who work in the diamond district. I get out as soon as I can in my bullet-proof car.

"For my own personal comfort, I'd like to stay in New York. I'm happy here. I like the weather, I like where I live, I like my milkman. But the ultimate consideration is, Are we going to be able to do the best, most competitive version of this show in New York or Los Angeles?"

The show premiered on schedule, with an estimated twenty-three million viewers watching.

It started with Larry "Bud" Melman, now known by his real name of Calvert DeForest, coming out of the CBS eye to tell viewers which network they were tuned to.

Then the star himself appeared and got right down to business.

"I would like to thank the good folks here at CBS for taking the low-key approach to promoting this show." The audience howled. After letting the laughter go on for a bit, Letterman smiled crookedly. "The Gulf War didn't get this kind of coverage. Ladies and gentlemen, this is not a promo—this is the *actual show!*"

Then he continued. "My name is Dave, and I have checked this with the CBS attorneys and legally I can continue using the name Dave."

He said that he wasn't really worried at all about NBC's threatened lawsuit over its "intellectual properties" because the network was "all tied up defending *Dateline: NBC*."

Letterman said he was puzzled about one thing, though. "This morning I woke up and next to me in bed was the head of a peacock."

Even then the "intellectual properties" subject would not go away. Tom Brokaw, the NBC news anchor and one of Letterman's favorite guests at NBC, came on the show and greeted him affably.

"Dave, big night for you. I wanted to come across the street and say hello, and, you know, wish you—well, wish you *reasonably* well. But I'm a little shocked. Frankly, Dave, I'm kind of *disappointed.*"

He reached out and grabbed up a couple of Letterman's cue cards. "Fact is, these last two jokes are the intellectual property of NBC!" And with that he walked off the set to cheers and laughter.

Letterman responded instantly: "Who would have thought that you would ever hear the words 'intellectual property' and 'NBC' in the same sentence? Stunning, isn't it?"

Soon Letterman introduced Paul Newman, who stood up in the audience and called out to Letterman:

"Where the hell are the singing *Cats?*" he asked, referring to the Broadway musical. When Letterman told him *Cats* was just down the street, Newman said, "I'm in the wrong theater!" and dashed up the aisle and out the door. To great applause and laughter.

Letterman confessed later that it was not *his* clout that got Paul Newman on the show, but the fact that Michael Ovitz, his agent, was a friend of Newman's. The joke was a memorable one not only for the jest itself but for the superstar who had delivered it.

Bill Murray reprised his role as Letterman's first guest on *Late Night* twelve years before. He started spray-painting the name "Dave" on Letterman's desk, but the paint gun jammed temporarily after he got the first two letters on. When he did finish the name DAVE he explained his purpose to his host in a typically Letterman squelch:

"There are a lot of people who still don't know who you are."

One of the most amusing segments of the show was a taped remote of Letterman out in the field asking people in a small community in New Jersey what new ideas they wanted explored on the show. No one seemed to know what he was talking about.

"Do you have any idea who you're talking to?" he asked one of the people he was interviewing.

"No."

"Bryant Gumbel," Letterman lied.

She had never heard of Gumbel. Obviously, she had never heard of Letterman either.

"Would you watch a television show that had naked people on playground equipment?" he asked.

The tape then showed a blurry picture of unidentifiable nudes.

All that segment proved was that humor of the ironic kind never did play well in America. Letterman's straight face and boyish look—even at his age!—threw off the unsuspecting. And yet, to the initiated, the irony of the segment was a pleasure to behold. The mixture of mainstream humor and sophisticated late-night stuff proved to be a welcome addition to the eleven-thirty audience tuned in.

Other features on the show included a child prodigy of four named Jonathan Estrada. His expertise at that age included geography. He showed how he could bite replicas of American states out of American cheese slices. *And* he could put in a tooth mark correctly to indicate the site of the state's capital!

The initial show even had a new Top Ten—this one titled "Top Ten Ways the New Show Will Be a Lot Better" (presumably, "Better than the Old One")

10. Kids watch free.
 9. No more relying on cheap G.E. jokes (unless we're really stuck).
 8. My new "Rappin' Dave" character.
 7. Inhaling asbestos particles from renovation makes me extra "wacky."
 6. If they applaud really loudly, everyone in tonight's studio audience gets a brand-new car!
 5. No more pressure to book NBC President Robert C. Wright's son-in-law, Marv Albert.

4. It's the same show. Better Time. New sta— Oh, for the love of God, stop staying that!
3. I'm more focused since my breakup with Loni.
2. Every Friday Paul [Shaffer] and I swap medication.
1. A whole new wardrobe for Vanna!

Next day, with tongue in cheek, NBC announced that it was quite happy with Tom Brokaw's visit to the Letterman show. "We are pleased that Tom Brokaw reclaimed our property last night. If David crosses the line, it might be necessary for Tom to return. We wish David Letterman well and look forward to the competition."

Almost lost amidst the guests and the jokes was the fact that David Letterman had appeared in a somewhat different garb from his NBC late-night appearances. He was dressed in a natty suit, with traditional shirt and tie.

He had made the decision to wear a suit "like a grown-up," he said, for a very good reason. "From the practical side, I get so tired of 'Do these pants go with this jacket? Does this tie?' And now you pretty much know the jacket and pants are going to go together. That's kind of a given. So it limited the decision-making ordeal."

CHAPTER SIXTEEN
On a Roll

The Late Show with David Letterman continued after its premiere with a number of very good follow-ups and some innovations that revealed intelligence and discernment among the staff and David Letterman.

One of the top shows in the new format occurred on the night of September 8, the second week of the *Late Show*. Letterman's guest was Al Gore, the Vice President of the United States.

It started out with a teaser, a scene supposedly backstage at the Ed Sullivan Theater, with Gore discussing some jokes with his talk-show host. Gore wanted to appear professional in his humor—not amateurish.

"How about, 'I'm so stiff that I went for a checkup and the doctors declared me legally dead'?" Gore wondered.

Letterman told him frankly that he did not think the "I'm-so-stiff-that" type of joke would be good for the Vice President.

"How about, 'Know what words are the President's favorite, the one he most likes to hear?' " Letterman countered.

Gore did not know.

" 'Would you like fries with that?' "

Letterman cracked himself up over that one, and laughed helplessly while Gore fumed.

"That's the President of the United States you're talking about!" he snapped.

All in fun.

The rest of Gore's appearance combined humor with some serious matters. He wanted to talk about the plan both President Clinton and he had for trying to overhaul government. And talk he did.

"So, have you fixed the government?" Letterman asked first off, getting some laughs from the audience.

Gore admitted that of course neither he nor the President had really begun.

As the two chatted briefly Letterman stumbled over the word "implementations" and Gore caught him up immediately on the faux.

"Beg pardon?" he asked. "What was that word?"

"Implementations," Letterman admitted, pronouncing it right that time.

Gore: "Don't make me check your spelling!" he added with a smile.

A rimshot from Paul Shaffer.

The Vice President demonstrated the kind of thing Clinton and he wanted to wipe out. He brought out what he called an "ash receiver, tobacco (desk type)" and then corrected himself quickly.

"Sorry. That's an ashtray!"

And then he explained that it was called ash receiver, tobacco (desk type) in the specifications.

What interested Gore was the way such an ashtray had to be broken in order to test it. "They have to count the number of pieces [it falls into]," he said, "and it can be no more than thirty-five pieces!"

And so he and Letterman put on safety goggles and brought out the ash receiver, tobacco (desk type) and proceeded to smash it into bits with a hammer. Of course they were forced to follow government instructions and pulverize it on a "maple plank" as mandated by the government.

When it was all done Letterman looked down at the fragments of the ashtray on his desk and chuckled dryly. "Cool," he said.

Before Gore left he recited his own Top Ten list, which he called "Top Ten Good Things about Being Vice President." The list follows:

10. Police escort gets you to the movies faster.
9. You know that game tetherball? I played tetherball with the inventor of tetherball.
8. After they sign a bill, there's a lot of free pens.
7. If you close your left eye, the seal on the podium reads "President of the United States."
6. I get intellectual property rights to my speeches.
5. Dan Quayle and Gerald Ford are pretty easy to beat during Vice Presidents' Week on *Jeopardy*.
4. You don't have to be funny to get invited on the Letterman show.
3. You get to eat all the french fries the President can't get to.
2. You don't have to be a good speller to get the job.

"And the Number One good thing about being Vice President," Gore said in conclusion: "Your Secret Service code name: Buttafuoco."

Another rimshot from Shaffer.

In October, it was someone who did not appear on the *Late Show* who caused Letterman to get a little unwanted publicity again.

A former Gambino mobster named Joseph (Joe Dogs) Iannuzzi had become an FBI informant and had been inducted into the federal witness-protection program. He had also written a cookbook for Simon & Schuster titled *The Mafia Cookbook*.

Several television talk-show hosts had invited Iannuzzi to appear to promote his new cookbook, but Iannuzzi had turned them down. U.S. marshals warned him that he would be booted out of the federal witness-protection program if he appeared on TV.

Letterman's staff invited Iannuzzi to appear on the show,

and Iannuzzi decided to act on his own. "Dave was my idol," he said. "I figured he was a real New Yorker—you know, a standup kind of guy."

Iannuzzi's people and Letterman's people scheduled a taping of a segment.

"I told my marshal," Iannuzzi said.

"You're out of the program the minute you leave home to go on the show," the marshal warned him.

Iannuzzi wanted to publicize his book, and boarded a plane to New York City.

"The marshals terminated me," he said. Then he showed up to tape the night's program as arranged. However, the producer of the segment told him the piece had been canceled.

"He won't go on the show with you. He's afraid."

Iannuzzi: "I called him every name in the book!"

At CBS, a highly placed spokesperson said that it was Letterman's staff that was concerned that the segment would not fit the show's format. They were the ones who canceled the segment. "Dave had nothing to do with the decision."

Iannuzzi had the last word.

"He thinks he's got a problem with that Margaret Ray showing up in his living room. Wait until he gets home one night and finds me waiting for him."

As the show progressed, it was clear that the new format fit Letterman perfectly. And it also fit the audience that was tuning in.

In late November, the ratings were proof positive that things were working out all right for Letterman. Since the start of the official television season in September, Letterman's *Late Show* averaged a 5.2 rating, translating into 4.8 million households. (Each point represents 942,000 homes.) That was a 79 percent increase over the one-hour crime dramas that CBS was programming in the same time slot the year before.

Jay Leno was averaging a 4.1 rating for the same time period, down 7 percent from the period a year before.

A new talk-show hosted by Chevy Chase on the Fox network, had averaged a 2.6 rating in its brief life.

Arsenio Hall was getting a 2.2 rating for his syndicated talk show in the same time period.

And ABC's *Nightline* was averaging a 4.9 rating for the same period, even though it was an entirely different kind of program.

Following Letterman in the 12:30 to 1:30 A.M. time slot, Conan O'Brien was drawing a 1.8 average rating.

One thing that stood out about the Letterman show was the fact that in the new time slot, for some reason he appeared to have become a better interviewer than he had been in the later time slot.

A Letterman watcher reported recently that he got Barbara Walters, for example, to comment approvingly on Clint Eastwood in jeans as seen from behind.

One of his guests had asked him during a casual conversation whether he was a Presbyterian or an Anglican, and Letterman thought a moment, and then replied.

"I'm just not sure."

What was sure was that whatever it was that made it so, the *Late Show with David Letterman* was taking on all comers and in general beating them handily.

Nor was Vice President Al Gore the only politician who appeared on the show and scored high with the viewers. During the inauguration ceremonies of Rudolph W. Giuliani, the newly elected mayor of New York City, Giuliani's son, Andrew—seven years old, going on eight (in a few days)—stood beside the lectern as his father spoke, and soon began mouthing the words he could see on the prompter before him.

His antics began to overshadow the important speech his father was giving. In fact, at one point Andrew spoke the words his father was going to say before the mayor was able to get them out.

The old show-biz admonition—never appear on stage with a child or a dog—proved true. Andrew became the star of the inauguration. And so the Letterman staff called up to ask the boy to appear on the *Late Show*. However, Mrs. Giuliani demurred. It would not be good for Andrew's school work.

Later, chatting with the mayor, Letterman suggested that the mayor himself should appear. Giuliani accepted the offer, since, he said, it would be a way to prove to the public that he could handle himself as well as his son could.

On the night of January 10, the newly elected mayor appeared on the show. At first he and his host discussed the antics of his son Andrew at length. Giuliani said that the boy had also accidentally spilled a pitcher of water on him—and had apologized profusely for doing so.

"I didn't know what this water was dripping down my leg," the mayor noted at one point.

"Well, I guess this is New York City," Letterman conceded. "It could be *anything.*"

The mayor then told a few jokes, using his scratchy Mafia voice in imitation of "Fat Tony" Salerno. Then the two of them went on to discuss matters of greater import.

Such as:

"The last time you talked about me," Giuliani said, "I think you said my hairpiece was sworn in the day after I was sworn in."

"That's right," Letterman said. "But you don't wear a hairpiece at all, do you?"

"No."

"But some people *think* you do."

"I know, I know. There's no hair left to even attach a hairpiece to."

They discussed the fact that Giuliani had refused to go on the Letterman show just after winning the election, with the excuse that he was "tired out."

As the two were chatting, a lookalike for Andrew Giuliani suddenly appeared outside the window before which Letterman sat at his desk and began mugging and making gestures with his hands in a spirited imitation of Andrew.

Those antics closed out the interview. In the end, when Letterman finally asked the mayor if Andrew would be watching the show that night—it was of course being taped several hours earlier—the mayor said:

"I think we'll tape it for him and let him watch it tomorrow."

By the beginning of the year 1994, the *Late Show* was on a roll. In an essay comparing Jay Leno, Johnny Carson, and

David Letterman, Steven D. Stark, a commentator for National Public Radio, made a number of interesting points about Letterman's humor—which he introduced as being "quintessentially New York."

"His humor is more pointed," he wrote, "more insulting, and almost always more ironic than Leno's. If Letterman is far more cynical than a Carson or a Leno, it's because world-weary New Yorkers aren't the optimists westerners are. If they were, they would have gotten in the wagon (covered or station) and left for greener pastures, too. New York jokes have an edgy undertone of 'Aren't we sophisticated?' with Letterman's foil often being Middle Americans—people who enjoy playing *Stump the Band.*

"Letterman's show also appears more spontaneous—in the tradition of vaudeville. In contrast, southern California late-night jokes are more like prime-time TV humor: If the laughter isn't canned, the jokes sure seem like they are. A Reagan, a Carson, and a Leno tell stories as much as they tell jokes. Their comedic tradition owes less to the Borscht Belt and more to the Western 'tall tale.'

"What's more, in the Paar tradition, Letterman is always the witty star, even if he's talking to a guest."

Stark concluded: "So it goes today. If everything breaks right for Letterman, American viewers may find New York a nice place to revisit for an hour a night. But they'll never stand for living there again."

In *Vogue* magazine, Robert E. Sullivan, Jr., discussed what he considered to be a great improvement in the new David Letterman: his ability to interview guests.

"The gradual growth of [Letterman's] skills as an interrogator indicates that he has long been pushing the interview-as-comedy envelope, and he is now simply moving along, becoming the Letterman who, with time, experimentation, and maybe his forties, he was bound to become."